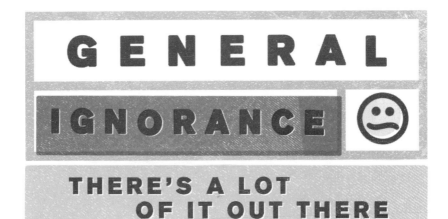

GENERAL IGNORANCE

THERE'S A LOT OF IT OUT THERE

Publications International, Ltd.

CONTENTS

INTRODUCTION

We've all fallen prey to it: the juicy rumor, the urban myth, a bland health tip, or commonsensical truism. It can be painful to discover that our cherished tidbit is incorrect, or, worse, one big accretion of illogic, innuendo, and gullible dissemination. Yet learning the truth often brings with it an "aha!" feeling. It might even inspire us to question our sources more thoroughly in the future.

This collection represents our attempt to shed light on the crackpot ideas, entrenched myths, con jobs, conspiracy theories, erroneous beliefs, and errant histories that always seem to sneak into life. Join us on this intellectual treasure hunt as we unearth origins, revel in the ridiculous, and question the truth behind a wide array of topics that includes:

- Who really dropped the apple on Isaac Newton
- Hitler's (non)vegetarianism
- The "poetic license" that created Paul Revere
- Toads and warts: an unjustified smear campaign

You're sure to come away with an amused sense of discovery that you can use to impress, educate, or discredit friends and acquaintances as you see fit!

War is God's way of teaching Americans geography.
—Unknown

It's not just Americans who need help with their road maps. Most past civilizations were guilty of a little fabrication and/or cluelessness when filling in the blanks between their equivalents of Topeka and Tulsa. We have flyover states. They had Atlantis. Most of us can't find El Paso on a map. They couldn't find El Dorado because it didn't actually exist.

To complicate things, there are plenty of misleading place names out there to throw off the unwary. The man who named Greenland was a liar. The West Indies are a case of wishful thinking. The Windy City has nothing on the breezy towns of Texas. And have you ever been to Pleasantville, New Jersey?

REWARD: ONE LOST ISLAND

It's hard to believe that Plato, an early Greek philosopher, was the type to start rumors. But in two of his famous dialogues, *Timaeus* and *Critias*, he refers to what has become one of the most famous legends of all time: the doomed island of Atlantis.

In *Timaeus*, Plato uses a story told by Critias to describe where Atlantis existed, explaining that it "came forth out of the Atlantic Ocean, for in those days the Atlantic was navigable; and there was an island situated in front of the straits which are by you called the Pillars of Heracles; the island was larger than Libya and Asia put together, and was the way to other islands." Not only that, but Plato also divulges the details of its fate: "afterwards there occurred violent earthquakes and floods; and in a single day and night of misfortune all your warlike men in a body sank into the earth, and the island of Atlantis in like manner disappeared in the depths of the sea. For which reason the sea in those parts is impassable and impenetrable, because there is a shoal of mud in the way; and this was caused by the subsidence of the island." In *Critias*, the story revolves around Poseidon, the mythical god of the sea, and how the kingdom of Atlantis attempted to conquer Athens.

Although many ascribe Plato's myth to his desire for a way to emphasize his own political theories, historians and writers perpetuated the idea of the mythical island for centuries, both in fiction and nonfiction. After the Middle Ages, the story of the doomed civilization was revisited by such writers as Francis Bacon, who published *The New Atlantis* in 1627. In 1870, Jules Verne published his classic *Twenty Thousand*

Leagues Under the Sea, which includes a visit to sunken Atlantis aboard Captain Nemo's submarine Nautilus. And in 1882, *Atlantis: The Antediluvian World* by Ignatius Donnelly was written to prove that Atlantis did exist—initiating much of the Atlantis mania that has occurred since that time. The legendary Atlantis continues to surface in today's science fiction, romantic fantasy, and even mystery stories.

More recently, historians and geologists have attempted to link Atlantis to the island of Santorini (also called Thera) in the Aegean Sea. About 3,600 years ago, one of the largest eruptions in recent history occurred at the site of Santorini: the Minoan, or Thera, eruption. This caused the volcano to collapse, creating a huge caldera or "hole" at the top of the volcanic mountain. Historians believe the eruption caused the end of the Minoan civilization on Thera and the nearby island of Crete, most likely because a tsunami resulted from the massive explosion. Since that time, most of the islands, which are actually a complex of overlapping shield volcanoes, grew from subsequent volcanic eruptions around the caldera, creating what is now the volcanic archipelago of islands called the Cycladic group.

Could this modern tourist hot spot truly be the site of the mythological island Atlantis? Some say that Plato's description of the palace and surroundings at Atlantis were similar to those at Knossos, the central ceremonial and cultural center of the Minoan civilization. On the scientific end, geologists know that eruptions such as the one at Santorini can pump huge volumes of material into the atmosphere and slump other parts of a volcanic island into the oceans. To the ancient peoples, such an event could literally be translated as an island quickly sinking into the ocean. But even after centuries of study, excavation, and speculation, the mystery of Atlantis remains unsolved.

THE HOLLOW EARTH GANG

For centuries, people have believed that Earth is hollow. They claim that civilizations may live inside Earth's core or that it might be a landing base for alien spaceships. This sounds like fantasy, but believers point to startling evidence, including explorers' reports and modern photos taken from space.

Hollow Earth believers agree that our planet is a shell between 500 and 800 miles thick, and inside that shell is another world. It may be a gaseous realm, an alien outpost, or home to a utopian society. Some believers add a spiritual spin. Calling the interior world Agartha or Shambhala, they use concepts from Eastern religions and point to ancient legends supporting these ideas.

Many Hollow Earth enthusiasts are certain that people from the outer and inner worlds can visit each other by traveling through openings in the outer shell. One such entrance is a hole in the ocean near the North Pole. A November 1968 satellite photo showed a dark, circular area at the North Pole that was surrounded by ice fields.

Another hole supposedly exists in Antarctica. Some Hollow Earth enthusiasts say Hitler believed that Antarctica held the true opening to Earth's core. Leading Hollow Earth researchers such as Dennis Crenshaw suggest that

President Roosevelt ordered the 1939 South Pole expedition to find the entrance before the Germans did.

The poles may not hold the only entrances to a world hidden deep beneath our feet. Jules Verne's famous novel *Journey to the Center of the Earth* supported yet another theory about passage between the worlds. In his story, there were many access points, including waterfalls and inactive volcanoes. Edgar Allan Poe and Edgar Rice Burroughs also wrote about worlds inside Earth. Their ideas were based on science as well as fantasy.

SCIENTISTS TAKE NOTE

Many scientists have taken the Hollow Earth theory seriously. One of the most noted was English astronomer Edmond Halley, of comet fame. In 1692, he declared that our planet is hollow, and as evidence, he pointed to global shifts in Earth's magnetic fields, which frequently cause compass anomalies. According to Halley, those shifts could be explained by the movement of rotating worlds inside Earth. In Halley's opinion, Earth is made of three separate layers or shells, each rotating independently around a solid core. We live on the outer shell, but the inner worlds might be inhabited, too. Halley also suggested that Earth's interior atmospheres are luminous. We supposedly see them as gas leaking out of Earth's fissures. At the poles, that gas creates auroras.

SCIENTISTS LOOK DEEPER

Hollow Earth researchers claim that the groundwork for their theories was laid by some of the most notable scientific minds of the 17th and 18th centuries. Although their beliefs remain controversial and unsubstantiated, they are still widely discussed among a network of enthusiasts.

Some researchers claim that Leonhard Euler (1707–1783), one of the greatest mathematicians of all time, believed that Earth's interior includes a glowing core that illuminates life for a well-developed civilization, much like the sun lights our world. Another mathematician, Sir John Leslie (1766–1832), suggested that Earth has a thin crust and also believed the interior cavity was filled with light.

In 1818, a popular lecturer named John Cleves Symmes, Jr., proposed an expedition to prove the Hollow Earth theory. He believed that he could sail to the North Pole, and upon reaching the opening to Earth's core, he could steer his ship over the lip of the entrance, which he believed resembled a waterfall. Then he would continue sailing on waters inside the planet. In 1822 and 1823, Symmes petitioned Congress to fund the expedition, but he was turned down. He died in 1829, and his gravestone in Hamilton, Ohio, is decorated with his model of the Hollow Earth.

PROOF GETS WOOLLY AND WEIRD

In 1846, a remarkably well-preserved—and long extinct—woolly mammoth was found frozen in Siberia. Most woolly mammoths died out about 12,000 years ago, so researchers were baffled by its pristine condition.

Hollow Earth enthusiasts say there is only one explanation: The mammoth lived inside Earth, where those beasts are not extinct. The beast had probably become lost, emerged into our world, and froze to death shortly before the 1846 discovery.

EYEWITNESSES AT THE NORTH POLE

Several respected scientists and explorers have visited the poles and returned with stories that suggest a hollow Earth.

At the start of the 20th century, Arctic explorers Dr. Frederick A. Cook and Rear Admiral Robert E. Peary sighted land— not just an icy wasteland—at the North Pole. Peary first described it as "the white summits of a distant land." A 1913 Arctic expedition also reported seeing "hills, valleys, and snow-capped peaks." All of these claims were dismissed as mirages but would later be echoed by the research of Admiral Richard E. Byrd, the first man to fly over the North Pole. Hollow Earth believers suggest that Byrd actually flew into the interior world and then out again, without realizing it. They cite Byrd's notes as evidence, as he describes his navigational instruments and compasses spinning out of control.

UNIDENTIFIED SUBMERGED OBJECTS

Support for the Hollow Earth theory has also come from UFO enthusiasts. People who study UFOs have also been documenting USOs, or unidentified submerged objects. These mysterious vehicles have been spotted—mostly at sea—since the 19th century.

USOs look like "flying saucers," but instead of vanishing into the skies, they plunge beneath the surface of the ocean. Some are luminous and fly upward from the sea at a fantastic speed . . . and without making a sound.

UFO enthusiasts believe that these spaceships are visiting worlds beneath the sea. Some are certain that these are actually underwater alien bases. Other UFO researchers think that the ocean conceals entries to a hollow Earth, where the aliens maintain outposts.

WHO LIVES AT THE ENDS OF THE EARTH?

Throughout history, people from every culture and walk of life have conjured images of far-off, mythical places with exotic names like Xanadu, Shangri-La, and Milwaukee. This universal desire to fantasize about unknown lands likely gave rise to such terms as "the four corners of the earth" and "the ends of the earth." These phrases suggest that somewhere on our plane of existence exist identifiable, ultimate nether regions—locations farther away from us than any other. A search of the King James Bible turns up no fewer than twenty-eight occurrences of the term "ends of the earth." Psalm 72:8, for example, reads, "He shall have dominion also from sea to sea, and from the river unto the ends of the earth." This is a translation of the Latin *Et dominabitur a mari usque ad mare, et a flumine usque ad terminus terrae*. At a time when guys in togas and sandals went around speaking to each other in Latin, most folks probably did believe that the earth was flat and really did have ends.

Today, most of us don't use the term so literally. It's relative and open to your imagination. The ends of the earth could mean the North Pole. If you live in Paris or Rome, perhaps it means the remote Amazon jungle. And if you live on a Himalayan peak, it might mean Milwaukee.

THE REAL DIRT ON THE DESERT

Sand dunes, scorching heat, mirages. If this is your image of the desert, you're in for a surprise. There are many stories about the desert that have spawned numerous myths. Here are two favorites.

IT NEVER SNOWS IN THE DESERT

Wrong. Believe it or not, the largest desert on Earth is Antarctica, where it snows a lot—the mean annual precipitation ranges from 5.9 to 10.2 inches. So why is Antarctica considered a desert? The definition of a desert is a region that receives very little *rain*. To be precise, a desert landscape exists where rainfall is less than 10 inches per year. Rain, of course, is needed to sustain certain types of plants and animals, but snow doesn't count as rain. So Antarctica—with all its wet snow—is dry enough to be considered a desert.

MOST SANDSTORMS OCCUR IN HOT, DRY DESERTS

It's true that dangerous sandstorms commonly occur in hot, dry deserts, including the Sahara and the Gobi. But they also occur frequently in a place you might never consider—North China, particularly around the area of Beijing. A ten-year research project found that sandstorms affecting China were closely related to the cold front from Siberia, according to the Inner Mongolia Autonomous Regional Meteorological Station. As the cold front swirls through the Gobi and other large desert areas, it often combines with cyclones in Mongolia, consequently bringing sandstorms to China. So if you're planning a trip to the Great Wall of China, prepare to dust yourself off!

HOW DO YOU GET TO OZ?

What, doesn't everyone know that Oz is somewhere over the rainbow? Is there a soul in the civilized world who hasn't traveled with Dorothy and Toto to that magical kingdom that was brought to life in the 1939 classic *The Wizard of Oz*? The young Dorothy (Judy Garland) and her beloved dog are whisked off their Kansas chicken ranch by that tornado and ultimately follow the Yellow Brick Road to Oz, where they meet the mighty wizard. Beyond the fantasy, though, why not pin down the actual physical location of Oz? Impossible, you say? No, indeed. First of all, we can rule out one state because Dorothy utters the famous line, "Toto, I've a feeling we're not in Kansas anymore."

So where could the tornado have tossed Dorothy and her pooch? Well, even assuming this was one of the most devastating twisters of all time—an F5 on the Fujita scale used by meteorologists—there's a limit to how far a human being can be carried by a tornado. According to researchers at the Tornado Project in St. Johnsbury, Vermont, small objects have whooshed great distances, but the farthest a human being has been thrown is about one mile.

So Dorothy couldn't have gone far—let's say a mile and a half because she was smaller than a full-grown adult. Therefore, Dorothy must have lived right on the Kansas border. And not out in the middle of nowhere, either, because at the start of the film, farm worker Hickory makes this statement: "But someday, they're going to erect a statue to me in this town."

So liftoff was near some kind of city or village right at the edge of Kansas. And you have to assume that Oz itself couldn't have been in an empty cornfield, either, because there would have needed to be some sort of population where Dorothy and Toto landed. Only the northern and eastern borders of Kansas provide search points, because most tornadoes move from southwest to northeast. A twister on either of the state's other two borders would have carried Dorothy and Toto further into Kansas.

There is only one location that fits the description provided in the movie. Dorothy's Uncle Henry and Aunt Em must have lived just outside of Atchison, Kansas—east of Highway 7 near the Missouri River—and the infamous tornado carried girl and dog little more than a mile to the outskirts of Rushville, Missouri—Oz.

Before you scoff, consider some curious coincidences. Tornado activity in the Rushville area is 143 percent greater than the overall U.S. average. Oh, and Atchison is the birthplace of Amelia Earhart. The gallant aviatrix, Atchison's most famous daughter if you aren't counting Dorothy, vanished on her flight around the world in 1937 but was declared dead in 1939—the same year *The Wizard of Oz* was released. Perhaps Amelia can be found over the rainbow.

THE ISLAND THAT
ISN'T AN ISLAND

Rhode Island isn't surrounded by water, so how the heck did it get its name?

NOBODY'S PERFECT

The history of exploration is, in some ways, a history of mistakes. Ponce de Leon blundered through the swamps of Florida because he believed that he was going to find the Fountain of Youth. Ferdinand Magellan believed that it would take only three days to sail from South America to Indonesia (try four months). And, of course, Christopher Columbus was so confused as to believe that a tiny island in the Caribbean was India.

To some extent, these mistakes are understandable—no European had been to the Caribbean previously—but others, not so much. For example, it would take a geographically challenged individual of the highest order to believe that a body of land bordered on only one side by water should be called an island. Yet that's precisely what the founders of Rhode Island seem to have done.

A quick glance at the map will tell you that islands do make up a chunk of Rhode Island's decidedly small landmass, though the vast majority of it lies on the continent, wedged between Massachusetts and Connecticut. And a quick glance at the Constitution will tell you that Rhode Island isn't the official name of the state at all. The official name is "The State of Rhode Island and Providence Plantations." How

Rhode Island got that name is almost as confusing as how a body of land the size of a postage stamp can be legitimately termed a state in the first place.

A COMEDY OF ERRORS

This whole mess may be the result of a misunderstanding. Some historians argue that Rhode Island was named by confused settlers who believed that they were living on a body of land that the 16th-century explorer Giovanni da Verrazzano likened to the Mediterranean Greek island of Rhodes; hence, they began calling their home Rhode Island. The only problem is that the island about which Verrazzano had waxed classical was a different island—the one that is now called Block Island.

The official story, though, is that Rhode Island got its name from the Dutch explorer Adriaen Block—he whose namesake island should actually be called Rhode—who called the region *Roodt Eylandt* ("Red Island") after the color of the local clay. When British settlers moved in, they anglicized the name to Rhode Island.

In 1636, Roger Williams, after being kicked out of the Massachusetts Bay Colony, founded his own settlement on the mainland beside Narragansett Bay. He named it Providence in the belief that divine intervention had led him there. Williams, a theologian who advocated tolerance and free thinking (neither of which had any place in the Massachusetts Bay Colony), eventually convinced settlers of the bay's islands—which included Rhode—to join him. The eventual State of Rhode Island and Providence Plantations was born, later shortened to Rhode Island by lazy Americans.

A GOOD LITTLE PLACE

Despite the series of blunders that led to its name, Rhode Island forged and maintains a reputation for culture and tolerance. The state was one of the first to pass laws banning slavery and one of only two that currently has laws allowing prostitution. Fourteen colleges and universities are crammed into its borders, and the Ivy League's Brown University is considered one of the finest educational institutions in the world. Its geography department, however, must be considered suspect.

ON TOP OF THE WORLD

Think you're at the top of the world when you climb Mt. Everest? Think again. You'll need to scale Ecuador's Mt. Chimborazo to make that claim.

You've scaled Mt. Everest and are marveling at the fact that you're getting your picture taken at the highest point on the planet. You're as close to the moon as any human being can be while standing on the surface of the earth!

Actually, you're not. To achieve that, you'd have to climb back down and travel to the other side of the world— Ecuador, to be exact—so you can schlep to the summit of Mt. Chimborazo.

It's true that Everest, at 29,035 feet, is the world's tallest mountain—when measured from sea level. But thanks to the earth's quirky shape, Chimborazo, which rises only 20,702 feet from sea level, is about a mile and a half closer to the moon than Everest's peak.

Earth is not a perfect sphere. Rather, it's an oblate spheroid. Centrifugal force from billions of years of rotating has caused the entire planet to flatten at the poles and bulge out at the equator.

In effect, this pushes the equator farther from the earth's center than the poles—about 13 miles closer to the moon. The farther you move from the equator, the farther you move from the moon. Chimborazo sits almost at the equator, while Everest lies about 2,000 miles north—enough to make it farther from the moon than Chimborazo, despite being more than 8,000 feet taller.

PASS THE SALT

When tourists float in the curative waters of the Dead Sea, they likely believe they are relaxing in the world's saltiest body of water. This is understandable, because just about every travel guidebook makes this claim—erroneously. But if you're determined to soak in the world's saltiest lake, you should skip the Dead Sea and head to Lake Asal in the tiny East African country of Djibouti.

Lake Asal's salinity measures 400 grams per liter—more than the Dead Sea's 340 grams per liter. Why is Lake Asal so salty? Salt lakes form in locations where water cannot flow away to the sea and is lost only through evaporation. Lake Asal was formed somewhere between 1 million and 4 million years ago, likely the result of volcanic activity and the resulting shift of Earth's surface. A crater lake 500 feet below sea level, Asal is fed only by underwater springs and is depleted only by evaporation. Consequently, the mineral salts have nowhere to go. Saline levels are so high that crusts of salt up to 13 inches thick accumulate at the lake's edge and are strong enough to withstand the weight of a car. There is no plant or animal life in the lake—nor on the land surrounding it.

Is that much salt a good thing? Lake Asal is not only extraordinarily salty but has the added distinction of being one of the least hospitable places on the planet. While the Dead Sea's buoyant, mineral-rich waters attract thousands of visitors annually, it is unlikely that Lake Asal will ever be a tourist destination. The air temperatures there are said to be unbearable and the glare from the salt blinding, and the lake itself emits a sulfurous stench.

If you still want to take a plunge, do so with your shoes on, because the salt-crystal crusts can rip bare feet to shreds. What's more, you'll come out of the water coated in a thick, salty film. Lake Asal is surrounded by a salt pan that is mined, and the salt is exported by caravan to Ethiopia.

FAKES, HOAXES, AND CONS

> **There's a sucker born every minute.**

P. T. Barnum, the consummate huckster, is popularly supposed to have said this. But have we misjudged America's Greatest Showman? Probably. The phrase has also been attributed to several late-19th-century sources, including con man Joseph "Paper Collar Joe" Bessimer and humorist Mark Twain.

What it means is that there's no shortage of human gullibility, and whoever said it was right (for the quote's most likely source, turn to page 103). Scams, schemes, and connivances appear in every corner of human history, and each generation obligingly provides a fresh crop of dupes and patsies for con artists to prey upon.

THE GREAT PIANO CON

Lauded late in life as a great piano virtuoso, British pianist Joyce Hatto produced the largest collection of recorded piano pieces in the history of music production. But were they hers?

Joyce Hatto was known as an extraordinary pianist. Her recorded repertoire available in the UK grew to more than 100 CDs and included some of the most difficult piano pieces around. What was truly amazing is that she somehow managed to record this music while suffering the effects of cancer and dealing with the usual wear and tear of an aging body. How did she do it? Perhaps her penchant for plagiarism helped. As it turned out, the majority of her works were stolen from other artists' recordings and then reproduced as her own!

Having enjoyed a full, albeit rather insignificant, career as a concert pianist, Hatto abandoned her stage show in 1976 to focus on her advancing disease. On the cusp of 50, she had only a few recorded numbers under her belt. However, that soon changed, as she spent her remaining years prolifically, but as it turned out, falsely, adding to that collection.

THE CD DELUGE BEGINS

That Hatto's husband, William Barrington-Coupe, ran the Concert Artists Recordings label under which her recordings were released undoubtedly helped to assist in the harmonious heist. His music business acumen provided both the technological savvy to engineer the pieces that had been previously released by other pianists and the means to unleash the forged works on an unsuspecting public.

Of course, the scam couldn't last forever. Internet rumors began surfacing in 2005, but *Gramophone*, a monthly music magazine in London, wasn't able to definitively break the news of the deception until February 2007, about eight months after Hatto's death. In fact, her death at age 77 may have actually been an impetus for the discovery.

After Hatto's passing, her celebrity fire burned hotter than ever. Beloved by a small fan base during her life, Hatto-mania came out in full force upon her death. Some even deemed her one of the great pianists of modern times. But with that superstar status came a renewed flurry of suspicions surrounding the likelihood of a woman of her age and ailing health being able to produce such a copious collection. *Gramophone* issued a summons for anyone who knew of any fraudulence. Months passed with no evidence, until a reader finally contacted the magazine to reveal his strange findings. As it turned out, this man's computer actually discovered the deceit.

THE CON REVEALED

Popping in a purported CD of Hatto hits, the reader's computer identified that a particular ditty was not a work of Hatto but one by little-known pianist Lazlo Simon. The reader immediately contacted *Gramophone* with his discovery. Based on his report, *Gramophone* sent the recordings to a sound engineer, who put music science to the test, comparing sound waves from Hatto's ostensible recording of Liszt's 12 Transcendental Studies to Simon's version.

An identical match was uncovered! After that, more and more tested pieces attributed to Hatto were found to belong to other musicians. Hatto and husband were able to manage the ruse by utilizing music technology to recycle others' recordings and reproduce them as Hatto's own; by that same technology, the deceptive duo was discovered. So, how could the pair not foresee that music science would reveal them, even as they used its wizardry themselves? Barrington-Coupe has not, as of yet, produced a viable answer.

Although he denied any wrongdoing at first, Barrington-Coupe eventually confessed to the fraud, defending his actions by insisting that Hatto knew nothing of the scheme and he had made very little money on it. He further claimed that the whole plot was inspired by nothing more than his love for his ailing wife and his attempt to make her feel appreciated by the music community during her final years. An assertion such as this can neither be proved nor disproved, but *Gramophone* pointed out that Barrington-Coupe continued to sell the false CDs after she had died.

PONZI: THE MAN AND THE SCAM

Do you want to get rich quick? Are you charming and persuasive? Do you lack scruples? Do you have a relaxed attitude toward the law? If so, the Ponzi scheme may be for you!

Yes, there was a real Mr. Ponzi, and here's how his scam works. First, come up with a phony investment—it could be a parcel of (worthless) land that you're sure is going to rise in value in a few months or stock in a (nonexistent) company that you're certain is going to go through the roof soon. Then recruit a small group of investors, promising to, say, double their money in 90 days. Ninety days later, send these initial investors (or at least some of them) a check for double their investment. They'll be so pleased, they'll tell their friends, relatives, neighbors, and coworkers about this sure-fire way to make a fast buck.

You use the influx of cash from these new investors to pay your initial investors—those who ask for a payout, that is. The beauty part is that most of your initial investors will be so enchanted with those first checks that they'll beg to reinvest their money with you.

Eventually, of course, your new investors will start to wonder why they aren't getting any checks, and/or some government agency or nosy reporter might come snooping around . . . but by then (if you've timed it right) you'll have transferred yourself and your ill-gotten gains out of the country and out of reach of the authorities. Like related scams that include pyramid schemes and stock bubbles, financial frauds like this one have been around for centuries, but only the Ponzi scheme bears the name of a particular individual—Charles Ponzi.

MR. AMBITION LEARNS HIS TRADE

As you might imagine—given that he was a legendary con man—Ponzi gave differing accounts of his background, so it's hard to establish facts about his early life. He was likely born Carlos Ponzi in Italy in 1882. He came to America in 1903 and lived the hardscrabble existence of a newly arrived immigrant. While working as a waiter, he slept on the floor of the restaurant because he couldn't afford a place of his own. But the handsome, suave Ponzi was determined to rise in the world—by fair means or foul. The foul means included bank fraud and immigrant smuggling, and Ponzi wound up doing time in jails in both the United States and Canada.

THE CHECK IS (NOT) IN THE MAIL

While living in Boston in 1919, the newly freed Ponzi more or less stumbled across the scheme that would earn him notoriety. It involved an easily obtained item called an International Postal Reply Coupon. In simple terms, the scam involved using foreign currencies to purchase quantities of a kind of international postal stamp, then redeeming the stamps for U.S. dollars. This brought in a handsome profit because of the favorable exchange rate of the time, and it actually wasn't illegal.

The illegal part was Ponzi's determination to bring ever-growing numbers of investors into the scheme . . . and just keep their money. Until the roof fell in, Ponzi became a celebrity. Before long, people across New England and beyond were withdrawing their life savings and mortgaging their homes to get in on the action.

The end came in the summer of 1920, when a series of investigative reports in a Boston newspaper revealed that the House of Ponzi had no foundations. By that time, he'd taken some 40,000 people for a total of about $15 million. Ponzi spent a dozen years in prison on mail fraud charges. Upon release, he was deported and continued his scamming ways abroad before dying—penniless—in Brazil in 1948.

THE COTTINGLEY FAIRY HOAX

It was a story so seemingly real that even the creator of the world's most intelligent literary detective was convinced it was true.

PIXIE PARTY

It was summertime in the English village of Cottingley in 1917 when cousins Elsie Wright and Frances Griffiths borrowed Elsie's father's new camera. When he later developed the glass plate negatives, he saw a photo of Frances with a group of four tiny, winged fairies. A prank, he figured. Two months later, the girls took another photo. This one showed Elsie with a gnome. At that point, her father banned them from using the camera again.

But a few years later, Wright's wife mentioned her daughter's fairy photos within earshot of theosophist Edward Gardner, who was so taken with them that he showed them to a leading photographic expert. After studying them extensively, this man declared the photos genuine. They caught the attention of spiritual believer Sir Arthur Conan Doyle, author of the Sherlock Holmes series, who published a magazine article announcing the Cottingley fairies to the world.

A DELUSIONAL DOYLE

In 1922, Doyle published *The Coming of the Fairies*. The book argued for the existence of fairies and contained the original photos along with three new pictures that Elsie and Frances had produced. Both the article and book ignited a pitched battle between believers and doubters. Many thought Doyle's fertile imagination had finally gotten the better of him.

FAIRY TALE?

As years passed, people remained fascinated by the story. In 1981, Elsie admitted that the whole thing was a hoax taken too far, and that the fairies were actually paper cutouts held up by hatpins. Frances, however, maintained the fairies were authentic even up to her death.

THE NONEXISTENT SPORTS STAR

A September 2002 issue of *Sports Illustrated* told of an unstoppable 17-year-old tennis force named Simonya Popova, a Russian from Uzbekistan and a media dream: 6'1", brilliant at the game, fluent in English, candid, busty, and blonde. She came from an appealing late-Soviet proletarian background and had a father who was often quoted in Russian-nuanced English. But she wouldn't be competing in the U.S. Open—her father forbade it until she turned 18.

The magazine verged on rhapsody as it compared Popova to Ashley Harkleroad, Daniela Hantuchová, Elena Dementieva, and Jelena Dokic. Editors claimed that, unlike Popova, all of these women were PR disappointments to both the Women's Tennis Association (WTA) and sports marketing because they chose to resist media intrusions to concentrate on playing good tennis. As a result, U.S. tennis boiled down to Venus and Serena Williams, trailed by a pack of hopefuls and won't-quite-get-theres. The gushing article concluded with this line: "If only she existed."

JUST KIDDING!

Popova *was* too good to be true. The biography was fiction, and her confident gaze simply showcased someone's digital artistry. Some people got it. Many didn't, including the media. They bombarded the WTA with calls: Who was Popova and why wasn't she in the Open? The article emphasized what many thought—the WTA was desperate for the next young tennis beauty. WTA spokesperson Chris DeMaria called the story "misleading and irritating" and "disrespectful to the great players we have." Complaining that some people didn't read to the end of articles, he said, "We're a hot sport right now and we've never had to rely on good looks."

Sports Illustrated claimed it was all in grand fun. It hardly needed to add that it was indulging in puckish social commentary on the sexualization of women's tennis.

THE ENIGMA OF THE CRYSTAL SKULLS

Once upon a time, a legendary set of crystal skulls was scattered across the globe. It was said that finding one of these skulls would bring the lucky person wealth . . . or death. The story also goes on to say that if all the skulls were located and placed together, they would begin to speak and reveal prophecies, including the end of the world. Could these skulls really exist?

THE HISTORY . . . MAYBE

Admittedly, the background of the crystal skulls is a little patchy. According to the legend, either the Aztecs or the Mayas hid 13 crystal human-size skulls around the world (though the number varies story to story). The skulls are said to possess supernatural powers, including the ability to speak as well as to heal, so perhaps they were hidden to prevent them from falling into the wrong hands.

Incredibly, several crystal skulls do exist—you can see even them in respected museums such as the British Museum and the Smithsonian. However, there is no documentation to support that any of the skulls were found during an excavation, or how they were found at all, for that matter. So where did they come from?

SELLING SKULLS
AND SEEING VISIONS

In the late 1800s, Eugene Boban was enjoying a successful career as a globetrotting antiques dealer. Boban is believed to have owned at least three of the crystal skulls, although it is unclear where he acquired them. However, two of these Boban skulls would end up in museums—one in the British Museum and one in Paris' Musee de l'Homme. But the most intriguing crystal skull is one that Boban did not own. This skull was discovered in 1924 by Anna Le Guillon Mitchell-Hedges, the adopted daughter of famed British adventurer F. A. Mitchell-Hedges. Anna claimed she found the skull in what is now Belize, inside a pyramid. Interestingly, her father wrote several books, but he never once mentions his daughter finding a crystal skull. Professional jealousy or did he regard the skull as a sham? Regardless, Anna claimed that the skull had magical powers and that she once stared into the skull's eye sockets and had a premonition of President John F. Kennedy's assassination.

PUTTING THE SKULLS TO THE TEST

Since the legends say that the skulls were hand carved, or a gift from the heavens (or aliens), scientists were eager to determine how they were formed. When the British Museum conducted tests on the two skulls they owned, they found marks that made it clear the skulls were carved using modern rotary tools. Likewise, Paris' Musée de l'Homme also found that their skull was created using modern tools. Both museums also discovered that the type of crystal used to form the skulls wasn't even available anywhere in the Aztec or Mayan empires.

At first, Anna Mitchell-Hedges was open to having the skull she found tested by the company Hewlett Packard (HP). They found that the skull was indeed crystal—and one solid block of crystal at that, which is incredibly difficult to carve, whether by hand or using modern machinery. Interestingly, Hewlett Packard also found that the quartz crystal is the same kind of crystal used in making computers.

THE LEGEND CONTINUES

Skeptics dismiss the crystal skulls as nothing more than a silly story. And it is an entertaining theory: Even director Steven Spielberg jumped on the bandwagon with his 2008 movie, *Indiana Jones and the Kingdom of the Crystal Skull*. True believers, on the other hand, firmly believe that just because the current skulls may be fakes, it doesn't mean the real skulls aren't still out there waiting to be found. And, say the believers, once all 13 are placed together in a room, the skulls will begin to speak, first to each other and then to anyone else who might be present. But until then, the crystal skulls are keeping their mouths shut.

I BURIED PAUL

In 1969, news broke that Beatles member Paul McCartney had died in a car crash three years before. The fantastic story claimed that McCartney's bandmates, stricken with fear that their popularity might wane, had installed a body double named William Campbell in Paul's place.

To stir up interest, the mop-tops allegedly left clues, such as a line at the end of "Strawberry Fields Forever," which uttered the words, "I buried Paul." The story had publicity stunt written all over it, but many still believed Paul was dead. A report by NBC anchorman John Chancellor summed things up: "All we can report with certainty is that Paul McCartney is either dead or alive."

Then, *Life* magazine discovered a very much alive Paul McCartney and snapped some photos. Confronted with the damning evidence, the clearly annoyed Beatle grudgingly granted *Life* an interview and the hoax was laid to rest.

The origin of the hoax remains unknown. Many believe the Beatles were directly involved since the boys had a penchant for mischief and a good joke. And to this day, there are some who still believe that William Campbell is standing in for Paul.

IT'S PROBABLY A CON IF . . .

From shell games to email scams, nearly all con games are played the same way: The "mark" gives up something of value to get a reward that never comes. Here are a few surefire signs that you're being conned.

- You trade money for something with questionable value. "The swap" is the heart of most cons. For example, a con artist might pose as a bank examiner, standing outside a bank. He flashes a badge, "inspects" a customer's withdrawn cash, and seizes the bills, claiming they are evidence in an embezzling case. He gives the customer a receipt and sends him or her back into the bank for replacement bills. When the mark goes back in, the con artist escapes.

- You pay for future money. This basic recipe is a con staple: You hand over your own money to access much more money. For example, in one scam, an email asks you to put up thousands of dollars to pay administrative fees that will unlock millions of dollars held overseas. Of course, after you wire your money, it disappears.

- A stranger trusts you. One way to earn someone's trust is to demonstrate trust in them first. For example, a con man might trust you to hold onto a diamond necklace he "found," if you put up a small fraction of what the necklace is worth (say, $200). A great deal . . . except the necklace is really a $5 knockoff.

- Someone else places their trust in the stranger. Many con games involve the use of a "shill," a co-conspirator who pretends to be like the mark. Seeing that someone else believes the con artist, the mark follows suit.

- You're running out of time. Con artists fog a mark's decision making by saying time is limited. The mark doesn't want to miss the opportunity and so throws caution to the wind.

- You're doing something bad. When the mark breaks societal rules, like taking found valuables rather than turning them in, he's less likely to go to the police after figuring out the scam.

THE HITLER DIARIES HOAX

Hitler may have been an ambitious politician but he wasn't much of a writer. After the success of *Mein Kampf*, the first volume of which was published in 1925 and the second in 1926, he seemed content to rest on his laurels, even if those laurels happened to be in a cramped cell in Landsberg prison. But surely such a significant historical figure would leave behind a greater written legacy than those two volumes? This apparent literary lethargy would eventually make some historians very gullible.

THE ROOTS OF THE HOAX

Though Hitler did halfheartedly pen a 200-page sequel to *Mein Kampf* in 1928, he grew bored with the project and never bothered to have it published. In fact, only two copies of the work existed, and those were kept under lock and key by Hitler's order. This manuscript was discovered by American troops in 1945, but though authenticated by several of Hitler's associates, it was considered to be both an inflammatory piece of Nazi propaganda and a dull rehash of *Mein Kampf*. For these reasons, the book was never published widely.

Hitler was quite literally a "dictator," relying on secretaries to take down his ideas and plans. Often, even Hitler's most grandiose and terrible commands—such as the one to completely destroy European Jewry—were given only verbally. Historians were also frustrated by the dearth of personal correspondence that could be linked to Hitler. His mistress, Eva Braun, was not the brightest woman to ever walk the face of the earth, and their correspondence has not been found.

FERTILE GROUND FOR A FAKE

This lack of primary-source material is part of what made the Hitler diaries hoax such a success at first. A staff reporter at West Germany's *Stern* magazine, Gerd Heidemann, fell for the ruse hook, line, and sinker, and believed the publication of the diaries would be a way of advancing his stalled career in journalism. He managed to convince his editors at *Stern* that the journals were legitimate, and they paid 9.3 million marks (about 6 million U.S. dollars at that time) for the first serial rights.

On April 25, 1983, *Stern* hit the streets with a sensational cover story: "Hitler's Diary Discovered." Media outlets around the world were more than happy to follow *Stern*'s lead, and the *New York Times*, *Newsweek*, and the *London Sunday Times* all immediately jumped on the huge story.

The editors at *Stern* certainly should have been more wary of Heidemann's story, as he was obsessed with Hitler and the Third Reich. He had a passion for acquiring Nazi collectibles of almost any sort, even emptying his bank account to buy Hermann Göring's dilapidated private yacht. However, Heidemann's enthusiasm was so contagious, and the demand for all things Hitler so great, that it seems his superiors simply couldn't resist. But from whom had Heidemann obtained the diaries? And where had they been all these decades?

FABRICATING THE FÜHRER

Konrad Kujau had started forging documents as a youth in East Germany, but he really hit his stride after defecting to West Germany and setting up an antiquities store in Stuttgart. Kujau was brazen and seemingly fearless in his work. He made and sold "genuine" Nazi items that sound ludicrous now and should have raised alarms for his clients then: Who could believe, for example, that Hitler had once written an opera? Yet his customers wanted to believe, and as long as Kujau shunned publicity, he was able to make a nice living off their ignorance and inexperience. After all, these were private collectors who wanted to hold onto their purchases as investments. But Kujau got greedy, and maybe just a little hungry for fame. Enter *Stern* reporter Heidemann, sniffing for a story.

Some time in 1981, Kujau showed Heidemann 62 volumes of what he claimed were Hitler's diaries, dated from 1932 to 1945. Heidemann was astonished and asked Kujau about their history; how had such important documents remained hidden and unknown for so many years? Kujau was ready with a plausible-sounding (to Heidemann, at least) explanation: Nazi flunkies had tried to fly Hitler's personal belongings, including the diaries, out of Berlin, but the plane had been shot down and crashed in Dresden, its cargo surviving without any major damage.

Conveniently for Kujau, Dresden was now behind the Iron Curtain, so his claim of obtaining the volumes one at a time from an East German general could not easily be confirmed or disproved. But if anyone longed to believe, it was Heidemann.

MEDIA CIRCUS

The publication of the diaries was an international bombshell, with historians, journalists, politicians, and antiquities dealers lining up to take sides in the subsequent media war. Some historians and scholars immediately pointed out Hitler's reputed aversion to writing in longhand, but others, such as the esteemed British World War II expert Hugh Trevor-Roper, declared the diaries to be authentic.

On the day the story was published, *Stern* held a press conference in which Trevor-Roper, along with German historians Eberhard Jackel and Gerhard Weinberg, vouched for the authenticity of the documents. It would be a mistake all three men would grievously regret.

The media uproar only intensified when, less than two weeks later, it was revealed beyond any question that the Hitler diaries were forged. Not only were the paper and ink modern, but the volumes were full of times and happenings that did not jibe with Hitler's known activities and whereabouts. Kujau was so careless in his fakery that he didn't even bother to get the monogram on the title page correct: It read FH rather than AH. Some observers pointed out that the German letters F and A are quite similar, but surely as a German himself, Kujau would have known the difference. The best guess is that the diaries were very sloppily prepared for his usual type of client—a dullish foreigner who wouldn't ask too many questions—and that Heidemann's arrival on the scene turned what might have been just another smooth and profitable transaction into a worldwide scandal.

OFF TO THE CLINK

Heidemann was arrested and tried for fraud, and Kujau was arrested and tried for forgery. Both men wound up serving more than four years in prison. Kujau reveled in his celebrity after his release, appearing on talk shows and selling paintings as "genuine Kujau fakes." But although Kujau tried to treat his crime as a lighthearted joke, it should be noted that had he not been unmasked, the diaries could have done real damage. Perhaps most serious—the document claimed that Hitler had no knowledge of the Holocaust.

SUPERSTITIONS AND MYTHCONCEPTIONS

> **If a black cat crosses your path, it signifies that the animal is going somewhere.**
> —Groucho Marx

Thanks, Groucho, our thoughts exactly. It's just an old superstition. All the same, we're still a bit reluctant to smell those dandelions, just in case they really do make you wet the bed.

Almost everyone is superstitious in their own way, whether they knock on wood, refuse to walk under ladders, or edge behind trees to avoid perniciously inky kitties. Sure, it's irrational and humiliating, but . . . well, that's pretty much all it is. Urban myths work the same way as superstitions: they infect a stupid host who then wanders around in search of another stupid host. Transmission accomplished, the contamination spreads.

THREE ON A MATCH

Let's start with an odd one that most of us are too young to remember, but which illuminates one of the ways peculiar superstitions can take life. The origins of the "three on a match" superstition is thought to have its genesis in the military. Like many superstitions, it is also based partially in reality: on a dark battlefield, a prolonged match flame can easily draw the attention of enemy snipers. Therefore, to light one cigarette is dangerous; to light three is to invite disaster.

Some historians believe this superstition started during the Boer War (1899–1902), when careless British soldiers became easy targets for Dutch sharpshooters by lighting up in the trenches. To be the third man in line for a light was extremely dangerous because you were likely already in the enemy's crosshairs by then.

Others believe that "three on a match" was started by Swedish match manufacturer Ivar Kreuger, who supposedly conceived the myth as a way of increasing sales during wartime. Kreuger certainly would have profited from this superstition, but there is very little evidence to suggest that the story is true.

What is true is that the history of superstition among soldiers dates back thousands of years, to the very first armed conflicts. "War is a situation in which you do everything possible to avoid being killed or your buddies being hurt, but so many things are out of your control," explains Dr. Stuart Vyse, author of *Believing in Magic: The Psychology of Superstition*. "Superstition gives service members the feeling that they are doing something that might have an effect—that they are taking some action to control a situation that is by definition uncontrollable. And that gives them comfort."

I WAS HANDLING THIS TOAD AND NOW I HAVE WARTS

Well you didn't get the warts from the toad—and he resents the implied accusation.

Toads have it bad enough without being blamed for the unsightly bumps we sometimes get on our skin. They're like the frog's ugly woodland-dwelling cousin, always playing second fiddle to those slick green amphibians. Kiss a frog and you'll get a prince; kiss a toad and you'll get an unsightly growth.

The myth that touching these creatures will give you warts might come down to nothing more than the similarity between warts and the bumps that serve as the toad's camouflage. It doesn't help that a good percentage of warts occur on people's hands, where contact between skin and toad is most likely to occur. But a toad's bumps are not warts; they're accumulations of mucus and poison glands in the toad's skin.

Another possible source of this myth has to do with these same poison glands. Upon making skin contact with a toad, some people have an allergic reaction to the natural toxins the toad excretes as part of its defense against predators. This reaction can cause a rash that might resemble warts. The key word here being resemble: This rash is not warts. Warts are actually caused by human papillomavirus (HPV), which is spread by contact. The virus enters through open wounds and mouth/eye contact. This means doorknobs, money, and faucets in public bathrooms should be treated as contaminated.

Washing your hands regularly will help you avoid contracting HPV and sprouting unsightly growths. If you do get a wart, keep it covered; HPV can spread over your own body through contact. Warts can be killed by a variety of over-the-counter remedies. Flash-freezing is a popular and time-tested technique. If you're patient, though, your immune system will generally eradicate the virus over time.

ROACH APOCALYPSE

The problem with the idea of cockroaches surviving nuclear war is not that it's untrue (it's true—they would). Rather, it makes them seem somehow more resilient than other small invertebrates. Cockroaches are indeed resilient. For one thing, they've spent millions of years surviving every calamity the earth could throw at them. Fossil records indicate that the cockroach is at least three hundred million years old. That means cockroaches survived unscathed whatever event wiped out the dinosaurs, be it an ice age or a giant meteor's collision with Earth.

Cockroaches can safely absorb a lot of radiation. During the Cold War, a number of researchers performed tests on how much radiation various organisms could withstand before dying. Humans, as you might imagine, tapped out fairly early. Five hundred Radiation Absorbed Doses (or *rads*, the accepted measurement for radiation exposure) are fatal to humans. Cockroaches, on the other hand, scored exceptionally well, withstanding up to 6,400 rads.

However, such hardiness doesn't mean that cockroaches will be the sole rulers of the planet if nuclear war breaks out. The parasitoid wasp can take more than 100,000 rads and still sting the heck out of you. Scorpions are incredibly hardy, as are ants, fruit flies, wood-boring beetles, and millimeter-long tardigrades. Some forms of bacteria can shrug off more than one million rads and keep doing whatever it is that bacteria do. Clearly, the cockroach would have neighbors.

Not all cockroaches would survive, anyway—definitely not the ones that lived within two miles of the blast's ground zero. Regardless of the amount of radiation a creature could withstand, the intense heat from the detonation would liquefy it. Still, the entire cockroach race wouldn't be living at or near ground zero—so, yes, at least some would likely survive.

Ultimately, if they're tiny and gross, they'll probably still be around.

AN INFAMOUS COMBINATION

How did Friday and 13 become forever linked as the most disquieting day on the calendar? It just may be that Friday was unlucky and 13 was unlucky, so a combination of the two was simply a double jinx. However, one theory holds that all this superstition came not as a result of convergent taboos, but of a single historical event.

On Friday, October 13, 1307, King Philip IV of France ordered the arrest of the revered Knights Templars. Tortured and forced to confess to false charges of heresy, blasphemy, and wrongdoing, hundreds of knights were burned at the stake. It's said that sympathizers of the Templars then condemned Friday the 13th as the most evil of days. No one has been able to document if this tale is indeed the origin of the superstition. And really, some scholars are convinced that it's nothing more than a phenomenon created by 20th-century media. So sufferers of paraskevidekatriaphobia (a pathological fear of Friday the 13th), take some comfort—or at least throw some salt over your shoulder.

CURSE OF THE TOMB

In the early 1920s, English archaeologist Howard Carter led an expedition funded by the Fifth Earl of Carnarvon to unearth the tomb of Egyptian King Tutankhamun. Most of the tombs of Egyptian kings had been ransacked long ago, but Carter had reason to believe that this 3,000-year-old tomb was still full of artifacts from the ancient world. He was right.

Carter had been warned about the dangers of disrupting an ancient tomb, but he didn't buy into the rumors of curses and hexes. After opening the tomb, however, it was hard to deny that some strange, unpleasant events began to take place in the lives of those involved in the expedition.

CURSE OR COINCIDENCE?

During the 1920s, several men involved in the excavation died shortly after entering King Tut's tomb. The first one to go—the Fifth Earl of Carnarvon—died only a few months after completing the excavation. Legend has it that at the exact moment the earl died, all the lights in the city of Cairo mysteriously went out. That morning, his dog allegedly dropped dead, too.

Egyptologists claim that the spores and mold released from opening an ancient grave are often enough to make a person sick or worse. The earl had been suffering from a chronic illness before he left for Egypt, which could have made him more susceptible to the mold, and, therefore, led to his death.

Other stories say that the earl was bitten by a mosquito. Considering the sanitary conditions in Egypt at the time, a mosquito bite in Cairo could have some serious consequences, including malaria and other deadly diseases. Some reports indicate that the bite became infected and he died as a result—not because an ancient pharaoh was annoyed with him.

There were other odd happenings, and the public, already interested in the discovery of the tomb itself, was hungry for details of "the curse of the pharaohs." Newspapers reported all kinds of "proof": the earl's younger brother died suddenly five months after the excavation, and on the morning of the opening of the tomb, Carter's pet bird was swallowed by a cobra—the same kind of vicious cobra depicted on the mask of King Tut. Two of the workers hired for the dig died after opening the tomb, though their passing was likely due to malaria, not any curse.

Six of the 26 explorers involved died within a decade. But many of those involved in the exploration lived long, happy lives, including Carter. He never paid much attention to the curse, and, apparently, it never paid much attention to him. In

1939, Carter died of natural causes at age 64, after working with King Tut and his treasures for more than 17 years.

King Tutankhamun's sarcophagus and treasures have toured the world on a nearly continual basis since their discovery and restoration. When the exhibit went to America in the 1970s, some people tried to revive the old curse. When a San Francisco police officer suffered a mild stroke while guarding a gold funeral mask, he unsuccessfully tried to collect compensation, claiming his stroke was due to the pharaoh's curse.

THE CURSE OF THE LOTTERY

Though many lottery winners live happily ever after, there are those whose "good luck" was nothing more than a prelude to tragedy—proving that money is not always the solution to social and personal ills, and giving credence to the old adage, "Easy come, easy go."

- At age 77, New Yorker Clarence Kinder won $50,000 in the state lottery on a Thursday night—and died from a heart attack the following night.

- Only a few hours after Carl Atwood won $57,000 on the televised lottery program *Hoosier Millionaire*, the 73-year-old was fatally hit by a pickup truck while walking to the store where he bought his winning ticket.

- Jeffrey Dampier won $20 million in the lottery and became a Tampa popcorn entrepreneur. Dampier's generosity to his sister-in-law, Victoria Jackson—gifts, apartment rent—evidently wasn't enough: Jackson and her boyfriend kidnapped and murdered Dampier for his fortune. They were sentenced to life in prison.

- After collecting the first of his annual $1.24 million checks, Billy Bob Harrell—a down-on-his-luck Texan who hit the state jackpot for $31 million—began spending like there was no tomorrow. He picked up a ranch, a fashionable home—and a never-ending line of family, friends, and even strangers with their palms outstretched, dogging him day and night. The spending spiraled out of control for 20 months, until Harrell, who had had quite enough, locked himself in his bedroom and let a shotgun solve his dilemma.

- William "Bud" Post won $16.2 million in the Pennsylvania lottery in 1988. When he died of respiratory failure on January 15, 2006, Post was living on a $450 monthly disability check and was estranged from his family. Not only was his fortune wiped out, but he ended up deeply in debt, and he served a jail term for threatening a bill collector with a shotgun. At one point, Post filed for bankruptcy, came out of it with a million dollars to his name, and spent it all in short order.

FEED A COLD, STARVE A FEVER

Don't worry if you can't remember whether you're supposed to feed a cold and starve a fever, or the other way around. Neither approach will cure you—but one could make you feel better.

No one knows for sure where this oft-repeated advice originally came from. But some myth busters have traced the adage back to the Middle Ages, when people believed illnesses were caused either by low temperatures or high temperatures. Those caused by low temperatures, including the common cold, needed fuel in the form of food, so eating was the treatment of choice. To the medieval mind, fever— or any other illnesses that caused a high temperature—was fueled by food, so the recommended treatment was to eat nothing or very little to help the body cool down.

Some evidence of this line of thought can be found in the writings of a dictionary maker named Withals, who in 1574 wrote, "Fasting is a great remedie of fever." But if it actually worked for people back then, it was probably a placebo effect.

Today, most medical experts (except for practitioners who promote fasting for healing) totally disagree with the notion of overeating or fasting to treat viral infections that cause colds and flu. When you have a cold or the flu, you actually need more fluids than usual. Drink plenty of water, juice, soup, and tea, and eat enough food to satisfy your appetite. Hot fluids will soothe a cough, ease a sore throat, and open clogged nasal passages. Food will supply nutrients that help bolster your immune system.

So stock up on chicken soup and tea and honey when the inevitable cold or fever strikes. And if a pint of mint chocolate chip ice cream helps you endure the aches and sniffles, why not indulge?

CURSED BLING

Diamonds are a girl's best friend, a jeweler's meal ticket, and serious status symbols for those who can afford them. But there's one famous diamond whose brilliant color comes with a cloudy history. The Hope Diamond is one of the world's most beautiful gemstones—and one that some say causes death and suffering to those who possess it. So is the Hope Diamond really cursed? There's a lot of evidence that says "no," but there *have* been some really strange coincidences.

THE ORIGIN OF HOPE

It's believed that this shockingly large, blue-hued diamond came from India several centuries ago. At the time, the exceptional diamond was slightly more than 112 carats, which is enormous. (On average, a diamond in an engagement ring ranges from a quarter to a full carat.) According to legend, a thief stole the diamond from the eye of a Hindu statue, but scholars don't think the shape would have been right to sit in the face of a statue. Nevertheless, the story states that the young thief was torn apart by wild dogs soon after he sold the diamond, making this the first life claimed by the jewel.

COURTS, CARATS, AND CARNAGE

In the mid-1600s, a French jeweler named Tavernier purchased the diamond in India and kept it for several years without incident before selling it to King Louis XIV in 1668, along with several other jewels. The king recut the diamond in 1673, taking it down to 67 carats. This new cut emphasized the jewel's clarity, and Louis liked to wear the "Blue Diamond of the Crown" around his neck on special occasions. He, too, owned the gemstone without much trouble.

More than a hundred years later, France's King Louis XVI possessed the stone. In 1791, when the royal family tried to flee the country, the crown jewels were hidden for safekeeping, but they were stolen the following year. Some were eventually returned, but the blue diamond was not.

King Louis XVI and his wife Marie Antoinette died by guillotine in 1793. Those who believe in the curse are eager to include these two romantic figures in the list of cursed owners, but their deaths probably had more to do with the angry mobs of the French Revolution than a piece of jewelry.

RIGHT THIS WAY, MR. HOPE

It is unknown what happened to the big blue diamond from the time it was stolen in France until it appeared in England nearly 50 years later. When the diamond reappeared, it wasn't the same size as before—it was now only about 45 carats. Had it been cut again to disguise its identity? Or was this a new diamond altogether? Because the blue diamond was so unique in color and size, it was believed to be the diamond in question. In the 1830s, wealthy banker Henry Philip Hope purchased the diamond, henceforth known as the Hope Diamond. When he died (of natural causes) in 1839, he bequeathed the gem to his oldest nephew, and it eventually ended up with the nephew's grandson, Francis Hope.

Francis Hope is the next person supposedly cursed by the diamond. Francis was a notorious gambler and was generally bad with money. Though he owned the diamond, he was not allowed to sell it without his family's permission, which he finally got in 1901 when he announced he was bankrupt. It's doubtful that the diamond had anything to do with Francis's bad luck, though that's what some believers suggest.

COMING TO AMERICA

Joseph Frankel and Sons of New York purchased the diamond from Francis, and by 1909, after a few trades between the world's most notable jewelers, the Hope Diamond found itself in the hands of famous French jeweler Pierre Cartier. That's where rumors of a curse may have actually originated.

Allegedly, Cartier came up with the curse concept in order to sell the diamond to Evalyn Walsh McLean, a rich socialite who claimed that bad luck charms always turned into good luck charms in her hands. Cartier may have embellished the terrible things that had befallen previous owners of his special diamond so that McLean would purchase it. Cartier even inserted a clause in the sales contract, which stated that if any fatality occurred in the family within six months, the Hope Diamond could be exchanged for jewelry valued at the $180,000 McLean paid for the stone. Nevertheless, McLean wore the diamond around her neck constantly, and the spookiness surrounding the gem started picking up steam.

Whether or not anything can be blamed on the jewel, it certainly can't be denied that McLean had a pretty miserable life starting around the time she purchased the diamond. Her eldest son died at age nine in a fiery car crash. Years later, her 25-year-old daughter killed herself. Not long after that, her husband was declared insane and was committed to a mental institution for the rest of his life. With rumors swirling about the Hope Diamond's curse, everyone pointed to the necklace when these terrible events took place.

In 1947, when McLean died (wearing the diamond) at age 60, the Hope Diamond and most of her other treasures were sold to pay off debts. Jeweler Harry Winston forked over the $1 million asking price for McLean's entire jewelry collection.

HOPE ON DISPLAY

If Harry Winston was scared of the alleged curse, he didn't show it. Winston had long wanted to start a collection of gemstones to display for the general public, so in 1958, when the Smithsonian Institute started one in Washington, D.C., he sent the Hope Diamond to them as a centerpiece. These days, it's kept under glass as a central figure for the National Gem Collection at the National Museum of Natural History. So far, no one's dropped dead from checking it out.

POP!
GOES YOUR STOMACH

Although eating the explosive candy Pop Rocks while drinking a soda isn't considered a healthful way to snack, it isn't fatal—despite what a persistent urban legend would have us believe.

In 1975, to the delight of bored little stinkers across the country, General Foods unveiled Pop Rocks, aka Space Dust. These tiny pebbles of vaguely fruit-flavored candy released a bit of carbonation when held on the tongue, causing a delightful "exploding" sensation.

DEATH BY POP ROCKS?

Although the candy was invented in 1956 (thus allowing ample time for testing), its startling novelty caused the Food and Drug Administration to set up a Pop Rocks hotline to reassure parents who were concerned about product safety. Despite these efforts, it became widespread playground knowledge that consuming the candy along with a carbonated beverage would cause one's stomach to explode. By 1979, the rumor was so pervasive that General Foods put full-page ads in 45 major-market publications, wrote more than 50,000 letters to school principals, and sent the inventor on a "goodwill tour" to debunk the myths. When General Foods stopped marketing Pop Rocks in 1983, many took it as proof that the confection was too dangerous to sell.

Adding fuel to Pop Rocks's fire was the widely rumored death of a child star who supposedly died after consuming a combination of the candy and soda. The kid, known to most only as "Mikey" (his character in a long-lived Quaker Life cereal commercial), was actor John Gilchrist. Although rumormongers claimed that Gilchrist mysteriously "disappeared" from the public eye after the commercial's 1972 debut (proof, of course, of his death), he actually continued making commercials through 1988 before retiring from acting. He is alive and well today, though talk of his unfortunate demise persists.

After General Foods stopped marketing the candy, Kraft Foods purchased the rights to it in 1983 and sold it under the name Action Candy. Today, Pop Rocks are back on the market under their original name, available for purchase online and in stores—without so much as a warning label.

Rumors about the candy have died down, likely due to the high-profile debunking it has received on TV shows and Web sites. However, in 2001, a lawsuit revived some of the original concerns. The suit was filed on behalf of a California girl who was rushed to a hospital in considerable pain after swallowing Pop Rocks that were blended into a special Baskin-Robbins ice-cream flavor. Doctors had to insert a tube into the child's stomach to help relieve gas pressure, but the ice cream was never determined to be the cause.

Despite that incident, Pop Rocks have enjoyed a revival, finding their way to the table as a mix-in for applesauce or yogurt and even as a garnish at retro-hip eateries. General Foods still holds U.S. patent number 4289794 for the "process of preparing gasified candy in which flavored sugar syrup—such as is used to make hard candy—is mixed with CO_2. The gas forms bubbles, each with an internal pressure of 600 pounds per square inch (PSI). As the candy melts on your tongue, the bubbles pop, releasing that pressure."

Although the thought of pressurized candy exploding into shards of crystallized sugar in your mouth or stomach sounds dangerous, it isn't. The amount of gas in a package of Pop Rocks is only one-tenth as much as there is in about an ounce of carbonated soda. Even if you combine Pop Rocks with a carbonated beverage, the pressure is not enough to make your stomach explode.

DON'T HOLD THE PEPPERONI

For years, spicy foods and stress took the rap for causing ulcers. The real culprit, however, has a Latin name.

You can have an ulcer and eat your pepperoni pizza, too. Research has proved that certain foods—including hot chilies, coffee, and curry—do not cause ulcers. Nor does stress, no matter how much you have to endure on the job or on the home front.

Your lifestyle is not to blame for the gnawing pain in your gut, though it can exacerbate your symptoms. Ulcers are most frequently caused by a bacterial infection. The little bug is called *Helicobacter pylori*, a corkscrew-shape bacterium that commonly lives in the mucous membranes that line the stomach and small intestine. Antibiotics are usually successful in eliminating such an infection.

Ulcers can also be caused by excessive use of nonsteroidal anti-inflammatory drugs (NSAIDs), such as ibuprofen or aspirin. That's because these medications inhibit the production of an enzyme that plays an important role in protecting your sensitive stomach lining.

Drinking alcohol and smoking, once also indicated as ulcer-causing habits, don't have primary responsibility for the development of ulcers, but they can be contributing factors. And they can definitely make an existing ulcer worse. Alcohol is an irritant that increases the amount of stomach acid you produce. The nicotine in cigarettes increases stomach acid, too, and prevents healing.

Don't confuse heartburn symptoms—burning, pressure, belching, and a bitter taste after eating—with those of an ulcer. Spicy foods can aggravate heartburn and gastroesophageal reflux disease (GERD), which are much more common than ulcers.

If you have ulcers, you don't have to worry about spicy foods. But if you have frequent heartburn, stay away from the chicken curry.

TAKE A SEAT

When your mother told you to sit up straight, she was off by about 45 degrees.

MOTHER USUALLY KNOWS BEST

Your mom was right when she admonished you to not slouch. But universal maternal advice about sitting perfectly straight can actually be harmful to your back's long-term health. That's right—when it comes to sitting up straight, you're advised not to listen to your mother.

Until recently, the long-standing conventional wisdom about sitting was that the back should be held ramrod straight, with thighs parallel to the floor. This posture was believed to protect the spine and cause the least amount of strain.

New research appears to have pulled the chair out from under this theory. It turns out that sitting upright for long periods of time can actually trigger chronic back pain.

Several studies have found that the once-recommended 90-degree sitting posture puts strain on the lower back. This position causes the disks between each vertebra to shift out of alignment. Over time, this can cause pain, deformity, and damage to the disks. And, as anyone who has tried to sit up straight for an extended period of time will tell you, it's just not very comfortable.

Experts now say it's best to sit with the chair back adjusted at a slight recline—a 135-degree angle—with your feet resting flatly on the floor. This position will reduce stress on the spine and it also causes the least amount of misalignment. Using this optimal position may help prevent back pain as well as treat it.

LUNA TICKS

A full moon holds mysterious attractions, prompting romantic outpourings, criminal malfeasance, lycanthropic tendencies, and boosted birthrates. Does the gleaming globe above our heads really have magical powers, or is it just our state of mind?

For many centuries, there have been reports of abnormal human behavior under the whole of the moon. Full moons have been linked to fluctuating rates of birth, death, crime, suicide, mental illness, natural and spiritual disasters, accidents of every description, fertility, and all kinds of irrepressible and indiscriminate howling. People with too much spare cash and not enough common sense have been known to buy and sell stocks according to phases of the moon. The word *lunatic* was coined to describe irrational and maniacal individuals whose conduct is seemingly influenced by the moon; their desolate domicile is dubbed the "loony bin."

DON'T BLAME IT ON THE MOON

So is there a scientific relationship between the moon and human behavior? In 1996, researchers examined more than 100 studies that looked into the effects of the moon—full or otherwise—on an assortment of everyday events and anomalies, including births and deaths, kidnappings and car-jackings, casino payouts and lottery paydays, aggression exhibited by athletes, assaults and assassinations, suicides and murders, traffic accidents and aircraft crashes.

Dr. Ivan Kelly, a professor of educational psychology and human behavior, found that the "phases of the moon accounted for no more than 3/100 of 1 percent of the variability in activities usually termed lunacy." This represents a percentage so close to zero that it can't be considered to have any theoretical, practical, or statistical interest. Because there was no significant correlation between the aforementioned occurrences and the periods and phases of the moon, it's safe to assume that the only moonshine that's causing trouble is the kind that's brewed in the Ozarks.

TOILET SEATS AND HERPES

Most people have no qualms about turning a doorknob, answering a telephone, or tapping out a to-do list on a computer keyboard. However, in a 2004 study sponsored by

Clorox, Charles Gerba, an adjunct professor of microbiology and immunology at the University of Arizona, found that such areas are many times "germier" than a toilet seat. In fact, a keyboard harbors almost seventy times more bacteria than a toilet, and a telephone has more than five hundred times as many germs. You may also consider that you probably will find more bacteria in a fast-food restaurant's ice than in its toilet, according to research performed by seventh-grader Jasmine Roberts, whose discovery made headlines in 2006. Add up all of this data, and it's nearly enough to make you believe that a toilet is a pristine environment.

Anyway, with that out of the way, let's quell the concern presented in the question: You cannot get herpes from a toilet seat. Says Rhoda Ashley, the director of the University of Washington's diagnostic virology laboratory at the Children's Hospital and Regional Medical Center in Seattle: "There has yet to be any documented cases of a person getting genital herpes from an inanimate object, such as a toilet seat or even a hot tub."

And what about oral herpes? Nope. Oral herpes, such as a cold sore or fever blister, is transmitted by touch between the contagious area and a cut or break in another person's skin and/or mucous membrane tissue, such as in the mouth, in the nose, or on the genitals.

So, even if you had way too much fun at the bar and woke up hugging the toilet bowl at some stranger's apartment, you can rest assured that you didn't contract herpes from the toilet seat. However, pubic lice, or "crabs," are another story. They can survive away from the human body for up to twenty-four hours.

COCA-COLA BURNED A HOLE IN MY STOMACH!

The world's most famous soft drink has been the subject of seemingly countless urban legends. One suggests that Coca-Cola can cause death from carbon dioxide poisoning, another says that it dissolves teeth, and still another posits that it makes an effective spermicide.

The topic here is whether Coke can burn a hole in your stomach. The answer is, quite simply, no. Your stomach is designed to withstand punishment—it's the Rocky Balboa of internal organs—and it can handle a lot worse than what little old Coca-Cola throws at it.

Your stomach takes every culinary delight that you consume and prepares it for the body to use as fuel. It breaks down food using hydrochloric acid—a substance that, in its industrial form, is used to process steel and leather, make household cleaning products, and even aid in oil drilling in the North Sea. Since this acid is highly corrosive, a mucus is secreted to protect the stomach lining.

The strength of an acid is measured on a pH scale that ranges from zero to fourteen. A pH level of seven is considered neutral; any substance with a pH level of less than seven is acidic. Where does your stomach's hydrochloric acid fall on the pH scale? Its pH level is one, meaning that it is among the most potent acids in existence. Coca-Cola contains phosphoric acid, a substance with a pH level of about 2.5. Phosphoric acid, then, is less potent than what is already inside you.

In other words, Coca-Cola isn't going to burn a hole in your stomach.

Still, there are some reasons to hesitate before you take the pause that refreshes. Coca-Cola contains the stimulant caffeine. (There is a caffeine-free Coca-Cola, but we're talking about the original version.) The stomach reacts to stimulants by creating more acid, which isn't an issue when the stomach is working well. But when the stomach contains ulcer-causing bacteria called *Helicobacter pylori*, the production of extra acid can exacerbate the problem. Further, people with gastroesophageal reflux disease (GERD) should avoid caffeinated drinks. And finally, phosphoric acid has been linked to osteoporosis. But under ordinary circumstances, a big swig of Coca-Cola isn't going to harm your stomach, or any other part of your body.

A CRITICAL MYTH

Contrary to a widespread rumor, famed film critic Gene Siskel did not insist that he be buried with his thumb pointing up.

Few in the specialized field of film criticism have been as well-known or respected as Gene Siskel, who penned countless movie reviews for the *Chicago Tribune* and later teamed up with fellow critic Roger Ebert of the *Chicago Sun-Times* on the popular television show *Siskel & Ebert.*

The show was famous for its movie rating system of "thumbs up/thumbs down," which became the duo's critical trademark. Shortly after Siskel's death in 1999 from complications following brain surgery, this story started to circulate: Among other provisions, Siskel's will stipulated that he be buried with his thumb pointing skyward.

Siskel's thumbs had made him internationally renowned, a legacy that he may have wanted to take to his grave. The rumor raced through the Internet in the form of a fake UPI news story that noted Siskel's unusual request. It read, in part: "According to public records filed in chancery court in Chicago, Gene Siskel asked that he be buried with his thumb pointing upward. The 'Thumbs Up' was the Siskel-Ebert trademark."

The story continued: "'Gene wanted to be remembered as a thumbs-up kind of guy,' said Siskel's lawyer. 'It wasn't surprising to me that he'd ask for that. I informed his family after his death, but he didn't want it made public until after his will had been read.'" The faux article carries all of the marks of a typical urban legend. Most telling is its failure to identify Siskel's attorney by name, which no legitimate news organization would do.

STICK AROUND

What happens if you swallow a stick of chewing gum? Will it stick around for seven years? Twist around your innards? Form a blockage in your digestive tract?

It's called chewing gum, not swallowing gum. But sometimes, accidentally or on purpose, a piece of gum ends up dropping down the gullet. When that happens, who hasn't wondered what the consequences will be?

No one knows how it got started, but the idea that swallowed chewing gum stays in the digestive system for seven years is a pervasive myth. It seems the misconception dates back thousands of years, as archaeologists have found evidence of ancient wads of chewing gum. Way back when, gum didn't come wrapped in paper and foil, but the concept was the same—it was something pleasant to chew on but *not* to swallow.

No matter how old the myth, you need not worry about swallowed gum taking up long-term residence in your stomach. Gastroenterologists say that inspections of the digestive tract, with exams such as colonoscopies and endoscopies, do not reveal clumps of petrified gum. When gum does show up on such scans, it is most often a recent arrival.

Although it's not intended to be ingested, chewing gum usually is not harmful if it ends up in your stomach instead of a trash bin (or under a desk). Some chewing gum additives, such as sweeteners and flavoring, are broken down by the body, but the bulk of gum is not digestible. Ingredients such as rubbery elastomers and resins remain intact during their slow voyage through the digestive tract. Eventually, the gum moves down and out.

In rare cases, an extremely large clump of swallowed gum could get stuck on its journey out of the body, causing a dangerous blockage. This potential problem can be avoided, however, if you chew just one stick at a time.

MYTHS ABOUT TORNADOES

It's a warm afternoon, and the skies have turned a greenish-gray color that can only mean trouble. Many misconceptions swirl around the subject of tornadoes. What many believe to be fact may actually be fiction.

The southwest corner of your house is the safest place to be during a tornado. In fact, occupying the area that is closest to the approaching tornado—whether it's above ground or in the basement—results in the most fatalities. A prominent study in the 1960s showed that the north side of a house is the safest area, both on the ground floor and in the basement. Many homes shift from their foundations during a tornado, toppling walls in the same direction as the storm's path. If the storm approaches from the southwest, then the home's southwest walls will fall into the structure, while north and northeast walls will fall away from the interior as the tornado moves away.

During a tornado, you should open all windows to equalize air pressure and reduce damage. The question of air pressure differences is really no question at all. Engineers agree that a storm with 260-mile-per-hour winds—classified as an F4, or "devastating," tornado—creates a pressure drop of only 10 percent. Homes and buildings have enough vents and natural openings to easily accommodate that. In fact, running around opening windows can increase the possibility of interior damage and personal injury, and it can take valuable time away from finding a safe place to ride out the storm.

A highway overpass is a safe place to wait out a storm when you're on the road. A clip of a TV news crew surviving a tornado by huddling under an overpass was seen around the world in the 1990s, leading many to believe this was a location out of harm's way. But most trained storm chasers consider highway overpasses extremely dangerous places to be when a tornado strikes. National Weather Service meteorologists judge overpasses to be poor shelters from severe weather because high winds essentially channel themselves under these structures, carrying with them flying debris.

Tornadoes never strike large cities. The following big cities (populations of at least 300,000) have witnessed tornadic activity: On a single day in 1998, three major tornadoes struck Nashville, Tennessee. St. Louis, Missouri, witnessed ten tornadoes between 1871 and 2007, resulting in more than 370 deaths. An F3 tornado roared through Dallas in 1957. In 1997, tornadoes touched down in Miami and Cincinnati, and another tore through Fort Worth, Texas, in 2000. Yet, this myth about large cities persists. The combination of traffic, dense activity, and considerable amounts of concrete and asphalt in large cities creates what is known as a "heat island." This rising warm air has the potential to disrupt minor tornadic activity, but it's no match for the fury of larger tornadoes. Cities occupy a much smaller geographic area than rural regions of the country, so the chance that a tornado will strike a city is relatively small.

You should use your vehicle to outrun a tornado. Experts say that you can try to drive away from a tornado—but only if it's a long way off. Tornadoes can travel as fast as 70 miles per hour and can easily overtake a vehicle. Even if a tornado is traveling at a much slower speed, the accompanying storm will likely produce strong winds, heavy rain, and hail that make driving difficult, if not impossible. What's more, tornadoes are dangerously erratic and can change directions without warning. If you're caught in a vehicle during a tornado, your best bet is to abandon it and seek shelter in a building or nearby ditch or culvert.

SNAKE FALLACIES

Fallacy: You can identify poisonous snakes by their triangular heads.
Fact: Many non-poisonous snakes have triangular heads, and many poisonous snakes don't. You would not enjoy testing this theory on a coral snake, whose head is not triangular. It's not the kind of test you can retake if you flunk. Boa constrictors and some species of water snakes have triangular heads, but they aren't poisonous.

Fallacy: A coral snake is too little to cause much harm.
Fact: Coral snakes are indeed small and lack long viper fangs, but their mouths can open wider than you might imagine—wide enough to grab an ankle or wrist. If they get ahold of you, they can inject an extremely potent venom.

Fallacy: A snake will not cross a hemp rope.
Fact: Snakes couldn't care less about a rope or its formative material, and they will readily cross not only a rope but a live electrical wire.

Fallacy: Some snakes, including the common garter snake, protect their young by swallowing them temporarily in the face of danger.

Fact: The maternal instinct just isn't that strong for a mother snake. If a snake has another snake in its mouth, the former is the diner and the latter is dinner.

Fallacy: When threatened, a hoop snake will grab its tail with its mouth, form a "hoop" with its body, and roll away. In another version of the myth, the snake forms a hoop in order to chase prey and people!

Fact: There's actually no such thing as a hoop snake. But even if there were, unless the supposed snake were rolling itself downhill, it wouldn't necessarily go any faster than it would with its usual slither.

Fallacy: A snake must be coiled in order to strike.

Fact: A snake can strike at half its length from any stable position. It can also swivel swiftly to bite anything that grabs it—even, on occasion, professional snake handlers. Anyone born with a "must grab snake" gene should consider the dangers.

Fallacy: The puff adder can kill you with its venom-laced breath.

Fact: "Puff adder" refers to a number of snakes, from a common and dangerous African variety to the less aggressive hog-nosed snakes of North America. You can't defeat any of them with a breath mint, because they aren't in the habit of breathing on people, nor is their breath poisonous.

Fallacy: Snakes do more harm than good.

Fact: How fond are you of rats and mice? Anyone who despises such varmints should love snakes, which dine on rodents and keep their numbers down.

DISNEY ON ICE

When his family shared only sketchy details of Walt Disney's death and next-day funeral with the media, a rumor germinated: He'd been cryonically frozen and was stashed under Pirates of the Caribbean at Disneyland.

According to records at St. Joseph's Hospital in Burbank, California, Walter Elias Disney died of lung cancer on December 15, 1966. On December 16, his studios announced that the funeral had already taken place at the Little Church of the Flowers in Forest Lawn Memorial Park in Glendale, California. There was a small, private funeral, followed by cremation and entombment on December 17.

The speedy ceremony raised a few eyebrows. Disney's daughter Diane had written years earlier that her father was neurotic about death. But because he hated funerals and didn't want one, his family simply honored his wish with a private burial. Months later, when a California psychologist underwent the first cryonic preservation, rumors began to swirl that Disney himself had been frozen.

Disney, a wealthy technophile, certainly could have afforded the expense of early cryonic preservation, but there is no evidence that he was particularly interested in the procedure. Records reveal that Disney's estate paid $40,000 for his burial plot, and his ashes rest at Forest Lawn—at the ambient temperature.

IT NEVER HAPPENED

> **Though God cannot alter the past, historians can.**
> —Samuel Butler

They can and they do. Herodotus (referred to by the ancients as "Father of History" except when they were calling him "Father of Lies") got the fibbing started with a whole string of anecdotal reports and thirdhand half-truths known, unironically, as *The Histories*. Among other whoppers, he claimed that the annual rise and fall of the Nile was due to the Sun being driven off course by storms, and that in northern Europe, a race of one-eyed barbarians passed the time looking for hoards of gold guarded by flying mountain lions. He also claimed that some ants grew as big as foxes—somewhere vaguely far away. And this, friends, is how history started. Are later historians any better? Sure, mostly. But that doesn't mean that a little deviant fibbery—accidental or otherwise—doesn't continue.

NEWTON'S APPLE

Could a falling apple have triggered one of the greatest scientific discoveries of all time? Probably not—but it's a cute story.

The tale of the apple landing on Isaac Newton's head during an afternoon nap has been told for hundreds of years as the explanation for his discovery of the law of gravity. If only it were so simple. Newton enjoyed taking walks in his orchard and probably even indulged in a nap or two under an apple tree. But his understanding of gravity did not come to him as a flash of insight. Rather, it was the result of years of painstaking study.

The Plague of 1665 probably had more to do with Newton's intellectual feat than a round red fruit. Newton was a 23-year-old student at Cambridge when the plague gripped England. As a result, the university closed and students were sent back to their homes in the countryside. Newton used this time to devote himself to his private studies, and in later years, he would refer to this period as the most productive of his life. He spent days working nonstop on computations and nights observing and measuring the skies. These calculations provided the seeds for an idea that would take years of covert and obsessive work to formulate—his Theory of Universal Gravitation.

Accounts of the apple story began appearing after Newton's death in 1727, probably written by the French philosopher Voltaire, who was famous for his wit but not his accuracy. He reported having heard the story about the apple from one of Newton's relatives, but there is no sound evidence to support that claim.

The falling apple will always be associated with Newton's great discovery. Many universities claim to own trees grown from grafts of trees from Newton's orchard, perhaps to remind overworked students that the theory of gravity was no piece of pie but, rather, the fruit of hard labor.

BRA BURNING: FROM MEDIA MYTH TO REVOLUTIONARY REALITY

In the late 1960s, the media reported that feminists were burning their bras at organized protests. The initial reports weren't true, but the label "bra-burning feminists" stuck.

FIERY FEMINISTS

In 1968, Robin Morgan and other influential feminist activists organized a protest of that year's Miss America beauty pageant. The demonstrators had considered burning bras and other symbols of the female beauty culture, but they decided this would be a fire hazard. Instead, they threw bras, girdles, handbags, and cosmetics into trash cans.

The mainstream media, however, got wind of the initial plan and inaccurately portrayed the hypothetical bra-burning incident as though it had actually happened. Doubtlessly titillated by the word *bra* and all it brings to mind, the male-dominated media began to report on bra burnings as though they were central to the feminist movement. Before long, "bra burners" became a catchphrase for radical feminists.

A STEREOTYPE GOES DOWN IN FLAMES

Historians and researchers have gone to great lengths to prove that there were no bra burnings at the famed protests. Many have interpreted the obsession with the idea as an attempt to reduce feminist politics into snide remarks about silly girls who torch their unmentionables. Although such bra-burning reductionism is sure to be found in many reports on the feminist movement, recent feminists have since taken up the media's reports and burned their own bras as the radical symbolic statement it was meant to be. Thus, though the famous bra burnings that the media reported never occurred, the spirit of creative destruction as a form of protest is not a myth.

IT'S RAMPANT SATANIC MARKETING!

What's behind the vicious rumor that put mega-corporation Procter & Gamble on many churches' hit lists?

Procter & Gamble, one of the largest corporations in the world, manufactures a plethora of products that range from pet food to potato chips. The company takes pride in its reputation as a business that can be trusted, so it came as a huge shock when, starting in the 1960s, Christian churches and individuals around the country spread the rumor that P&G was dedicated to the service of Satan.

THE DEVIL IS IN THE DETAILS

How the rumor got started remains a mystery. According to one of the most popular versions of the story, the president of P&G appeared on *The Phil Donahue Show* in March 1994 and announced that, because of society's new openness, he finally felt comfortable revealing that he was a member of the Church of Satan and that much of his company's profits went toward the advancement of that organization. When Donahue supposedly asked him whether such an announcement would have a negative impact on P&G, the CEO replied, "There aren't enough Christians in the United States to make a difference."

There's one problem with this story—and with the variations that place the company president on *The Sally Jessy Raphael Show*, *The Merv Griffin Show*, and *60 Minutes*: It didn't happen.

LOSE THE LOGO

Adding fuel to the fable was the company's logo, which featured the image of a "man in the moon" and 13 stars. Many interpreted this rather innocuous design to be Satanic, and some even claimed that the curlicues in the man's beard looked like the number 666—the biblical "mark of the Beast." By 1985, the company had become so frustrated by the allegations that it had no choice but to retire the logo, which had graced P&G products for more than 100 years.

SPEAKING OUT

Procter & Gamble did all it could to quell the rumors, which resulted in more than 200,000 phone calls and letters from concerned consumers. Company spokespeople vehemently denied the story, explaining in a press release: "The president of P&G has never discussed Satanism on any national televised talk show, nor has any other P&G executive. The moon-and-stars trademark dates back to the mid-1800s, when the "man in the moon" was simply a popular design. The 13 stars in the design honor the original 13 colonies."

In addition, the company turned to several prominent religious leaders, including evangelist Billy Graham, to help clear its name, and when that didn't work, it even sued a handful of clergy members who continued to spread the offending story. Talk show host Sally Jessy Raphael also denied the allegations, noting, "The rumors going around that the president of Procter & Gamble appeared on [my] show and announced he was a member of the Church of Satan are not true. The president of Procter & Gamble has never appeared on *The Sally Jessy Raphael Show*."

SENSELESS ALLEGATIONS

Of course, like most urban legends, this story falls apart under the slightest scrutiny. Foremost, one must ask why the CEO of an international conglomerate (especially one that must answer to stockholders) would risk decades of consumer goodwill—not to mention billions of dollars in sales—to announce to the world that his company was run by and catered to Satanists. And even if that were the case, he needn't bother announcing it, since any deals made with the devil would be a matter of public record.

AN OVERTURE TO WILLIAM TELL

Using his archery skills, William Tell shot an apple off his son's head. Right? Well, maybe not. Let's go over the legend again.

In 1307, Austria's Hapsburgs wanted to clamp down on the Swiss. An Austrian official named Hermann Gessler put his hat atop a pole and then made a petty, ridiculous rule: All passersby had to bow to his hat. An expert crossbowman named William Tell refused to bow, so Gessler's police arrested him. But Gessler wasn't satisfied with that. In a fit of sadistic illogic, Gessler made a deal with Tell. If Tell could shoot an apple off Tell's son Walter's head with the crossbow, both would be free. If Tell whiffed, or nailed his son, Gessler would execute him. Tell hit the apple but couldn't resist a snarky comment to Gessler. The latter, not renowned for his *joie de vivre*, got mad and threw Tell in jail. Eventually, Tell escaped and assassinated Gessler. This touched off a rebellion that led to the Swiss Confederation (which is still in business today, operating banks and ski lifts).

Where's the controversy?

To begin with, there is no contemporary historical evidence for Tell or Gessler. The legend first appeared in the late 1400s, and no one can explain the delay. What's more, the motif of an archer shooting a target off his son's head, then slaying a tyrant, appears in diverse Germanic

literature predating 1307. It's not that the William Tell
legend is necessarily false, because we can't prove it. The
combination of faults—lack of evidence, duplication of older
legends—makes the William Tell story a tough sell as history.

How do the Swiss feel about it? It wasn't easy for Swiss
patriots to carve out and hold their own country with all
the warlike tides of Europe buffeting them. The multilingual
Swiss have built and maintained a prosperous Confederation
that avoids warfare from a position of strength. William Tell
symbolizes Swiss love of freedom and disdain for tyrants,
domestic or foreign.

THE BEATLES' ODE TO LSD

Sure, the lyrics are trippy, but despite what the flower power
generation speculated (and many still believe), "Lucy in the
Sky with Diamonds" is not a song about LSD. The third track
on the Beatles' magnificent album *Sgt. Pepper's Lonely
Hearts Club Band*, was released in April 1967. That was the
beginning of the so-called Summer of Love, when hippies,
freaks, and counterculture types were experimenting with all
kinds of mind-expanding hallucinogens, including the trip-
inducing drug lysergic acid diethylamide, or LSD.

To some chemically altered minds, "Lucy in the Sky with
Diamonds" was a cleverly coded reference to LSD,
evidenced by the first letter of each of the key words in the
song's title. Furthermore, believers were convinced that John
Lennon's evocative lyrics and airy vocals were the perfect
musical expression of an acid trip. The myth of "Lucy in the
Sky with Diamonds" as the Beatles' ode to LSD was born.

Each of the Beatles has readily admitted to using acid during this period in their lives, but all of them have denied that "Lucy in the Sky with Diamonds" was inspired by the drug. The true inspiration for the song, as consistently stated by Lennon, was a drawing made by his then-four-year-old son, Julian, depicting a little girl surrounded by twinkling stars. The drawing, Julian explained to his father, was of his schoolmate Lucy O'Donnell—who was floating through the sky among diamonds. Lennon said the image reminded him of Lewis Carroll's *Through the Looking-Glass*, which in turn inspired the lyrics in the iconic Beatles song.

"Lucy in the Sky with Diamonds" isn't, as many believe, a song about LSD. Given the context of the times, however, it's not inconceivable that Lennon dropped a hit while writing it.

HITLER THE CLOSET CARNIVORE

Have you ever seen a photograph of Hitler enjoying a Bavarian sausage? The answer is likely no, but it's not because he was a vegetarian.

Adolf Hitler wanted the world to believe he was a vegetarian. This was propaganda—part of his image as a superhuman "aesthetic." He would publicly abstain from alcohol, tobacco, and womanizing so as to seem above all weaknesses. He often brought up his vegetarian diet in conversations and speeches, touting its virtues and predicting that Germany would eventually be a meat-free society. But Hitler was never a strict vegetarian.

Hitler drank alcohol (he used it to fall asleep), and he kept a mistress (Eva Braun). He also relished sausages and ham, and he had a weakness for caviar. When he began to suffer from an array of digestive problems, he was advised to take breaks from eating meat. Many of his doctors were actually quacks who prescribed a strange assortment of vitamin injections and fasting regimens. This was most likely the real reason for his occasional vegetarian diet.

But the myth of Hitler's vegetarianism has persisted. Tired of that name being included in their ranks, vegetarian activists have done much to unearth actual instances of Hitler eating meat. One of these is an excerpt from a 1960s German cookbook in which the author writes that "roast squab" was Hitler's favorite dish at a hotel where she'd worked. Apparently, he couldn't get enough of it. *Leberknödel* (liver dumplings) were another of his favorites.

A clear demonstration of Hitler's hypocrisy was the fact that he banned vegetarian societies in Germany. Those who met openly to discuss the philosophy of vegetarianism risked imprisonment or worse. There have been many famous vegetarians throughout history, but Adolf Hitler was not one of them.

AN UNCALLED-FOR SHOT?

Did the Babe call it?

This much is known. The Yankees had already won the first two games of the '32 fall classic when they met the Cubs at Wrigley Field for Game 3. Although Chicago players were understandably frustrated, there was bad blood between the teams that extended beyond the norm. In August, the Cubs had picked up former Yankee shortstop Mark Koenig from the Pacific Coast League to replace injured starter Billy Jurges, and Koenig hit .353 the rest of the season. Despite these heroics, his new teammates had only voted him a half-share of their World Series bonus money—a slight that enraged his old colleagues. The Yanks engaged in furious bench-jockeying with their "cheapskate" opponents the entire series, and Chicago players and fans shouted back, jeering that Ruth was old, fat, and washed-up.

When Ruth stepped up to bat in the fifth inning of Game 3, the taunts started as usual. A few people threw lemons at Babe from the stands, and he gestured toward the crowd before settling in at the plate. Charlie Root's first pitch was a called strike, and Ruth, looking over at the Chicago dugout, appeared to hold up one finger—as if to say, "That's only one." He did the same thing with two fingers after taking the second pitch, another strike. Then, some eyewitnesses recalled, he pointed toward dead center field. Others didn't remember this act, but there was no mistaking what happened next: Ruth slammed Root's third offering deep into the edge of the right-field bleachers. Onlookers recalled him laughing as he rounded the bases. And, as shown in a much-published photo, he and on-deck batter Lou Gehrig laughed and shook hands back at home plate.

What really happened? Here is where the facts end and speculation begins. Those among the 49,986 fans on hand who noticed Ruth's display likely assumed it was just another round in the ongoing feud between the two clubs, and most sportswriters made nothing out of it in their accounts of New York's 7–5 victory. The homer was not a game-winner; it was just one (in fact, the last) of 15 home runs Ruth hit in World Series play during his career. He had already taken Root deep earlier in the same contest, and Gehrig also had two in the game. The Yanks finished their four-game sweep the next day.

This being Babe Ruth, however, it only took a few speculative accounts from among the many reporters present to get the ball rolling. "Ruth Calls Shot" read the headline in the next day's *New York World Telegram*, and soon sports fans everywhere were wondering. Gehrig claimed he heard Ruth yell to Root, "I'm going to knock the next one down your goddamned throat" before the fateful pitch, while Cubs catcher Gabby Hartnett recalled the remark as "It only takes one to hit." Root and Cubs second baseman Billy Herman denied any gesture to the outfield, and grainy film footage that surfaced in 1999 was unclear either way. Ever the diplomat, Ruth himself granted some interviews in which he substantiated the claim, and others in which he denied it.

FIVE EXAMPLES OF TOTALLY UNTRUE HISTORY

LADY GODIVA'S NAKED RIDE

Even if the Internet had existed during the Middle Ages, you wouldn't have been able to download nude pictures of Lady Godiva because she never actually rode naked through the streets of Coventry, England. Godiva was a real person who lived in the 11th century and she really did plead with her ruthless husband, Leofric, the Earl of Mercia, to reduce taxes. But no records of the time mention her famous ride. The first reference to her naked ride doesn't appear until around 1236, nearly 200 years after her death.

SIR WALTER RALEIGH'S CLOAK

The story goes that Sir Walter Raleigh laid his cloak over a big mud puddle to keep Queen Elizabeth I from getting her feet wet. Raleigh did catch the queen's attention in 1581 when he urged England to conquer Ireland. The queen rewarded him with extensive landholdings in England and Ireland, knighted him in 1584, and named him captain of the queen's guard two years later. But an illicit affair with one of the queen's maids of honor in 1592 did him in. He was imprisoned in the Tower of London and ultimately beheaded for treachery. The story of the cloak and the mud puddle probably originated with historian Thomas Fuller, who was known for embellishing facts.

CINDERELLA WORE GLASS SLIPPERS

Ask anyone and they'll tell you that Cinderella wore glass slippers to the ball, but historians say that part of the legend isn't true. More than 500 versions of the classic fairy tale exist, dating back as far as the 9th century. In each account, Cinderella has a magic ring or magic slippers made of gold, silver, or some other rare metal, which are sometimes covered with gems but are never made of glass. In the earliest French versions, Cinderella wore *pantoufles en vair* or "slippers of white squirrel fur." In 1697, when French writer Charles Perrault wrote "Cendrillon," his version of the tale, the word vair had vanished from the French language. Perrault apparently assumed it should have been verre, pronounced the same as vair, but meaning "glass." Even a wave of the fairy godmother's magic wand couldn't make that mistake disappear, and it has been passed down ever since.

ABNER DOUBLEDAY INVENTED BASEBALL

Contrary to popular belief, Abner Doubleday did not invent the game of baseball. In 1907, a committee was formed to document how baseball had originated. The committee concluded that in 1839, as a youngster in Cooperstown, New York, Abner Doubleday drew a diamond-shaped diagram for a game he called "Town Ball." A great story, but merely a myth—especially considering Doubleday was attending West Point in 1839 and was never known to follow the game he supposedly invented. Today, it is generally accepted that Alexander Joy Cartwright, a New York bank teller and talented draftsman, invented the game. A plaque in the Baseball Hall of Fame credits him as "the Father of Modern Baseball," while Abner Doubleday has never been enshrined.

BEN FRANKLIN DISCOVERED ELECTRICITY

Benjamin Franklin did not discover electricity when his kite was struck by lightning in 1752. In fact, electricity was already well known at the time. Instead, Franklin was trying to prove the electrical nature of lightning. During a thunderstorm, as Franklin flew a silk kite with a metal key near the end of the string, he noticed the fibers on the line standing up as though charged. He touched the key and felt a charge from the accumulated electricity in the air, not from a lightning strike. This was enough evidence to prove his theory that lightning was electricity. Had the kite been struck by lightning, Franklin would likely have been killed as was Professor Georg Wilhelm Richmann of St. Petersburg, Russia, when he attempted the same experiment a few months later.

DID NERO FIDDLE WHILE ROME BURNED?

Over the ages, the phrase "Nero fiddled while Rome burned" has become a euphemism for heedless and irresponsible behavior in the midst of a crisis. But as a matter of historical fact, legend has it wrong.

In AD 64, much of Rome burned to the ground in what is known as the Great Fire. According to legend, the reigning emperor, Nero, purposely set the blaze to see "how Troy looked when it was in flames." From atop a palace tower, he played his fiddle and sang as the fire raged and consumed two thirds of the empire's capital.

Nero, a patron of the arts who played the lyre, wrote poetry, and fancied himself a great artist, often performed in public, challenging the beliefs of Rome's political class who believed such displays were beneath the dignity of an emperor. But music was, in fact, the most dignified of Nero's interests. Under the influence of a corrupt adviser who encouraged his excesses, his life became a series of spectacles, orgies, and murders. A few months after his first public performance, the Great Fire ravaged Rome for five days. Roman historian Suetonius, who hadn't even been born at the time of the fire, describes Nero singing from the Tower of Maecenas as he watched the inferno. Dio Cassius, a historian who lived a hundred years later, places him on a palace roof, singing "The Capture of Troy."

However, the historian Tacitus, who actually witnessed the fire, ascertained that the emperor was at his villa in Antium, 30 miles away. Many contemporary historians agree that Nero was not in Rome when the fire broke out (and there's no denying the fact that the fiddle wasn't really invented until the 16th century). According to Tacitus, Nero rushed back to Rome to organize a relief effort and, with uncharacteristic discipline and leadership, set about rebuilding and beautifying the city he loved.

SPACE GHOSTS

Shortly after the Soviet Union launched Sputnik 1 *on October 4, 1957, rumors swirled that several cosmonauts had died during missions gone horribly wrong, and their spacecraft had drifted out of Earth's orbit and into the vast reaches of space.*

It was easy to believe such stories at the time. After all, the United States was facing off against the Soviet Union in the Cold War, and the thought that the ruthless Russians would do anything to win the space race—including sending cosmonauts to their doom—seemed plausible.

However, numerous researchers have investigated the stories and concluded that, though the Soviet space program was far from perfect and some cosmonauts had in fact died, there are no dead cosmonauts floating in space.

According to authors Hal Morgan and Kerry Tucker, the earliest rumors of deceased cosmonauts even mentioned their names and the dates of their doomed missions: Aleksei Ledovsky in 1957, Serenti Shiborin in 1958, and Mirya Gromova in 1959. In fact, by the time Yuri Gagarin became the first human in space in April 1961, the alleged body count exceeded a dozen.

SPACE SPIES

So prevalent were these stories that no less an "authority" than *Reader's Digest* reported on them in its April 1965 issue. Key to the mystery were two brothers in Italy, Achille and Giovanni Battista Judica-Cordiglia, who operated a homemade listening post with a huge dish antenna. Over a seven-month period, the brothers claimed to have overheard radio signals from three troubled Soviet spacecraft:

- On November 28, 1960, a Soviet spacecraft supposedly radioed three times, in Morse code and in English, "SOS to the entire world."

- In early February 1961, the brothers are alleged to have picked up the sound of a rapidly beating heart and labored breathing, which they interpreted to be the final throes of a dying cosmonaut.

- On May 17, 1961, three people were allegedly overheard saying, in Russian, "Conditions growing worse. Why don't you answer? We are going slower . . . the world will never know about us."

THE BLACK HOLE OF SOVIET PR

One reason rumors of dead cosmonauts were so believable was the extremely secretive nature of the early Soviet space program. Whereas the United States touted its program as a major advance in science and its astronauts as public heroes, the Soviet Union revealed little about its program or the people involved.

It's not surprising, then, that the Soviet Union did not report to the world the death of Valentin Bondarenko, a cosmonaut who died tragically in a fire after he tossed an alcohol-soaked cotton ball on a hot plate and ignited the oxygen-rich chamber in which he was training. He died in 1961, but it wasn't revealed publicly until 1986. Adding to the rumors was the fact that other cosmonauts had been mysteriously airbrushed out of official government photographs. However, most had been removed because they had been dropped from the space program for academic, disciplinary, or medical reasons—not because they had died during a mission. One cosmonaut, Grigoriy Nelyubov, was booted from the program in 1961 for engaging in a drunken brawl at a rail station (he died five years later when he stepped in front of a train). Nelyubov's story, like so many others, was not made public until the mid-1980s.

Only one Soviet cosmonaut is known to have died during an actual space mission. In 1967, Vladimir Komarov was killed when the parachute on his *Soyuz 1* spacecraft failed to open properly during reentry. A Russian engineer later acknowledged that Komarov's mission had been ordered before the spacecraft had been fully debugged, likely for political reasons.

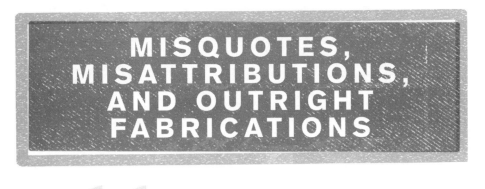

MISQUOTES, MISATTRIBUTIONS, AND OUTRIGHT FABRICATIONS

> **Quote me as saying I was misquoted.**
> —Groucho Marx

Admit it. Sometimes an embellished tale keeps them glued to their barstools longer. The game plan becomes a masterpiece. Last night's date gets hotter. The neighbor's children grow even longer tails. So it goes when humans are in charge of things like history, religion, and journalism.

Politics is where it gets really messy. Don't even think of trying to keep the story straight when it involves a hero or political opponent. Making hash of your enemy's words and spreading the resulting nonsense is a time-honored way of contributing flavor to the banquet of public discourse.

And sometimes getting it wrong just makes better copy.

"LET THEM EAT CAKE"

Most people recognize this dismissive remark as a slight uttered by the supremely snooty Marie Antoinette. Did the queen really say it? As it turns out, she didn't.

It's 1789, and the French Revolution is under way. Peasants are rioting in the streets, protesting a shortage of bread. Their queen, Marie Antoinette, not only ignores their hungry cries but flippantly feeds them a wisecrack. If there's no bread to be found, Her Haughtiness reasons, "Let them eat cake."

In French, the original quote is "Qu'ils mangent de la brioche," in reference to a type of bread characterized by a sweet flavor and flaky texture. Perhaps the queen was simply suggesting that her subjects not limit themselves to their usual staple and that they consider other forms of sustenance—like, well, *fancy* bread.

In fact, historians maintain that the line had nothing to do with the queen. Records show that it had been used in print to highlight aristocratic abuses since at least 1760. Philosopher Jean-Jacques Rousseau (who died more than a decade before the French Revolution began) claimed to have heard it as early as 1740. Even if such evidence didn't exist, the utterance of such a remark seems out of character for Marie Antoinette. According to biographer Lady Antonia Fraser, the queen had certain faults, but she wasn't tactless. "It was a callous and ignorant statement," explains Fraser, "and she [Marie Antoinette] was neither." Fraser believes the remark was actually made by Queen Marie Thérèse (wife of Louis XIV) nearly a century before the revolution began.

So why is the remark attributed to Marie Antoinette? Most historians believe propaganda played a big part. During the revolution, turning people against the queen was almost sport, and Marie endured plenty of scorn until her public beheading in 1793.

"DISSENT IS THE HIGHEST FORM OF PATRIOTISM"

So said Thomas Jefferson, according to bumper stickers and T-shirts worldwide. The problem is that this quote didn't exist twenty years ago, let alone in the 18th century.

Thomas Jefferson would be impressed by the wildfire spread of his latest alleged sound bite. Tracing this misquote's proliferation is like watching somebody trip in slow motion—you see it happening but aren't sure if the person's reflexes are a match for the inevitability of gravity.

During an interview on July 3, 2002, American historian and social scientist Howard Zinn defended his opposition to the war on terror by arguing "Dissent is the highest form of patriotism. In fact, if patriotism means being true to the principles for which your country is supposed to stand, then certainly the right to dissent is one of those principles."

Zinn appears to be the originator of this quote, and it quickly popped up in political speeches and newspaper articles as a defense for opposition to the war in Iraq. That would have been the end of it, had the quote not become a nexus for Republican versus Democrat warfare. Republican bloggers picked up on the quote's false source and attacked Senator John Kerry for misattributing it to Jefferson in a 2006 antiwar speech. Since then, so many journalists have debunked the misquote that it just may eventually be salvaged and properly sourced as a Zinn quote. As for Jefferson, he would have wanted nothing to do with the affair, as he explained in a letter he wrote in 1797: "So many persons have of late found an interest or a passion gratified by imputing to me sayings and writings which I never said or wrote . . . that I have found it necessary for my quiet and my other pursuits to leave them in full possession of the field."

THE QUOTABLE NATHAN HALE

In 1776, Revolutionary War hero Nathan Hale was hanged by the British for espionage. Is it true that his last words were "I only regret that I have but one life to lose for my country"?

Those are noble words worthy of a brave Continental officer. No knowledgeable historian would call them inconsistent with Nathan Hale's character: He was a volunteer who dared a dangerous task, conducted himself like a gentleman after capture, and went bravely to the noose. His character isn't being questioned, but did he actually utter the immortal words?

The evidence for the traditional quote comes from a British officer, Captain John Montresor, who told it to Hale's friend William Hull. The quote sounds paraphrased from Act IV of Joseph Addison's inspirational play *Cato*, one of Hale's favorites: "What pity is it, that we can die but once to serve our country!" (In addition to this quote, Patrick Henry's popular proclamation "Give me liberty or give me death" derives from Addison's play.)

Hale may have said the words, or something like them. Or Hull may have revised or misheard them, or Montresor may have gotten them wrong in the first place. There were only a few eyewitnesses, and versions didn't take long to begin wandering. Revolutionary-era media printed several variants on the theme, all of which make Hale sound like a valiant martyr.

What is beyond doubt: Hale was captured and legally executed as a spy. Before he died, he gave a rousing oration befitting a Yalie and a die-hard Continental patriot. This didn't stop his captors from putting him to death, but it did inspire them to tell the story, speak his name with respect (which British officers did not often do of their colonial counterparts), and describe him as a hero.

"RUM, SODOMY, AND THE LASH"

Is it possible that Prime Minister Winston Churchill, whose favorite port in a storm was any one with abundant alcohol, would dish out a disparaging dictum about the British Royal Navy?

When Great Britain was a dominant naval power, it was said that Britannia ruled the waves with a navy rich in resources and bathed in tradition. Therefore, it came as a shock to the British population when it was widely reported that Winston

Churchill was of the opinion that the only true traditions that the Royal Navy observed were "rum, sodomy, and the lash."

In fact, Churchill's dissenters perpetrated the origin of this myth-quote. In the 1940s, while he was serving as prime minister and his country was fighting for its very survival, Churchill's political foes concocted a smear campaign that focused on his apparent disdain for the navy. According to Churchill's competitors, young Winston had been denied entry to the Royal Naval College because he suffered from a speech impediment, and the scars of that snub never healed.

That wound still riled him when he allegedly rose in the House of Commons and delivered a scathing speech that ridiculed the Royal Navy and its traditions, which he summarized as the equivalent of alcohol, sex, and torture. But the entire incident proved to be fabricated. Records show that Churchill never attempted to join the navy, and documents concur that he never used the House of Commons as a platform to voice his opinions on the Admiralty. Yet, the line remains one of the most popular quotes attributed to Churchill. Its fame was cemented when he supposedly confided to his assistant, Anthony Montague-Browne, that although he had never spoken those words, he certainly wished he had.

IS THAT A CIGAR IN YOUR POCKET?

Did Freud really say, "Sometimes a cigar is just a cigar?" Seems plausible. Thanks to Sigmund Freud, penis envy and Oedipal complexes are common fodder for awkward conversations the world over. The Austrian psychiatrist, considered "the father of psychoanalysis," made popular the idea that your mind can hide its true desires, which are revealed only if you examine dreams and other subconscious thoughts for symbolism.

What a relief to hear that Freud, the ultimate over-thinker, might have admitted that sometimes an object has no hidden meaning.

In most retellings, this apocryphal anecdote occurs during a lecture on one of his pet topics, such as phallic imagery. An audience member cheekily asks what Freud's omnipresent cigars represent (wink, wink), causing the doctor to pronounce, "Sometimes a cigar is just a cigar."

Although Freud's fondness for cigars is well documented—he smoked 20 a day—there is no record he ever wrote or uttered the phrase. It is not included in his official papers, personal letters, or memoirs, nor is it mentioned in his daughter's biography. Even the curators of the Freud Museum in London can't verify it.

The quotation has a long history in comedy and is often linked with cigar-wagging Groucho Marx doing an imitation of Freud. On the other hand, folklorists relate the saying to Rudyard Kipling's poem *The Betrothed*, which reads, "And a woman is only a woman, but a good cigar is a smoke." But Freud might have said, if he had been the type to say such things, "Sometimes a pithy saying is just a pithy saying."

KISS AND MAKEUP

Why were protective parents around the globe convinced that the name of the rock band KISS was really an acronym for Knights in Service of Satan?

BRANDING A BAND

Onstage, they looked like they'd come straight from the gates of hell, dressed head-to-toe in black, their faces adorned with macabre makeup. When KISS hit the concert circuit in 1973—the group drew a sitting-room-only crowd of three people to their first gig—rock and roll was undergoing an image transformation. The emergence of androgynous rockers such as David Bowie and Marc Bolan, along with the popularity of glam groups such as Mott the Hoople and the New York Dolls, forced bands to find new, exciting, and controversial methods to market their product. When four young rockers from New York City decided to combine comic book characters and colorful costumes with a morbid mentality, they needed an appropriate handle to describe themselves, one that was easy to spell and mysterious enough to keep their fans confused. Drummer Peter Criss had been in a group called Lips, which prompted the crew to dub themselves KISS.

WHAT'S IN A NAME?

According to the boys in the band, the name was spelled in capital letters to make it stand out and was never meant to be an acronym for anything. But that revelation didn't stop members of religious flocks, who considered rock and roll to be synonymous with the sounds of Satan, from claiming that the group's moniker was a devilish derivation. In fact, the KISS name has spawned several acronymic identities, including Keep it Simple, Stupid; Kids in Satan's Service; and Korean Intelligence Support System. Judging from the millions of records they've sold in their 35 years in the business, as well as their relentless licensing of KISS-related merchandise, a more appropriate name for the band might be CASH.

LINCOLN DEFENDS GRANT

During the Civil War (1861–65), after hearing complaints of General Ulysses S. Grant's hard-drinking ways, did Abraham Lincoln really say, "For heaven's sake, find out what he drinks, and make the rest drink it, too"? Lincoln certainly had reason to make such a comment, and not the obvious one. His generals frustrated him, and he was always trying to kick their butts toward battle (preferably against the rebels rather than one another). Despite many Union advantages, the Confederacy habitually paddled the bluecoats until fighters such as Grant and Sherman put steel into the Union army's spine. What if jealous rivals were simply feeding a rumor mill?

There's an assumption that Grant was a drunkard to begin with. As a junior officer (1854), he did have a drinking problem and left the service because of it. In his Civil War return, he seemed to have learned his limits. Brigadier Grant made rapid gains in reputation, rank—and enemies. Numerous credible eyewitness accounts describe Grant as a moderate drinker, never intoxicated on the battlefield—something that can't be said of other leaders.

CELEBRITY TABLOIDS: HOW DO THEY GET AWAY WITH IT?

Supermarket tabloids thrive on publishing outlandish celebrity rumors and innuendo. You'd think that the subjects of their articles would be suing them all the time. How in the world could the tabloids survive the legal fees and multi-million-dollar judgments? The truth is, if tabloids are good at one thing, it's surviving.

There are two kinds of tabloids: the ridiculous ones that publish stories nobody really believes ("Bigfoot Cured My Arthritis!") and those that focus on celebrity gossip. The ridiculous stories are easy to get away with. They're mostly fabricated or based on slender truths. As long as they contain nothing damaging about a real person, there's no one to file a lawsuit. Bigfoot isn't litigious.

Celebrity gossip is trickier. To understand how tabloids avoid legal problems, we need to learn a little bit about the legal definition of "libel." To be found guilty of libel, you must have published something about another person that is provably false. Moreover, the falsehood has to have caused that person some kind of damage, even if only his or her reputation is harmed. If the subject of the story is a notable person, such as a politician or a movie star, libel legally occurs only if publication of the falsehood is malicious. This means that the publisher knows the information is false, had access to the truth but ignored it, and published the information anyway.

Tabloids generally have lawyers on staff or on retainer who are experts in media law and libel. By consulting with their lawyers, tabloid editors can publish stories that get dangerously close to libel but don't quite cross the line. One defense against libel is publication of the truth: You can't sue someone for saying something about you that's true, no matter how embarrassing it may be. And tabloids know that if they print something close to the truth, a celebrity is unlikely to sue because a trial could reveal a skeleton in the closet that's even more embarrassing.

Libel lawyers also know that a tabloid is in the clear if it publishes a story based on an informant's opinion. Opinions can't be disproved, so they don't meet the criteria for libel. This explains headlines such as this: "Former Housekeeper Says Movie Star Joe Smith Is a Raving Lunatic!" As long as the tabloid makes a token effort to corroborate the story—or even includes a rebuttal of the housekeeper's claims within the article—it is fairly safe from a legal standpoint.

Of course, legal tricks don't always work. Some movie stars, musicians, and other celebrities have successfully sued tabloids for tens of millions of dollars. That tabloids continue to thrive despite such judgments shows just how much money there is to be made in the rumors-and-innuendo business.

"THE BRITISH ARE COMING!"

Thank you Henry Wadsworth Longfellow for mangling this bit of colonial history.

Henry Wadsworth Longfellow's once-famous poem, "Paul Revere's Ride" begins with the lines, "Listen, my children, and you shall hear / Of the midnight ride of Paul Revere." He then proceeds to lay a whopper on generations of unsuspecting American schoolchildren. Let's sort through the misconceptions that have accreted around the liberty-loving equestrian from Boston.

Revere was half French. True. His mother was a Bostonian, and his father was a French immigrant named Apollos Rivoire. Anglicized to "Revere."

Revere was a brilliant silversmith. Not quite. He was certainly competent, and a good metalworking businessman, but he was no Michelangelo of silver. When history started venerating Paul Revere, it was a package deal: All his activities were magnified, logic and proportion aside.

Revere hung signal lanterns in a church tower. False. He had others hang them. Paul excelled at getting people to help his underground communications network. By the way, the actual signal was two dimly lit lanterns, which meant that the British army would take the Charles River route.

Revere yelled, "The British are coming!" False. That would be like someone from Indianapolis yelling, "The Americans are coming!" Like nearly all colonists, Revere considered himself British. His warning specified that the "regulars" (i.e., the regular British army) were on the march—which they were. Furthermore, it's unlikely that Revere "yelled" anything, because British army patrols were everywhere. That said, quietly muttering "the regulars are footing it hither!" just doesn't have the same punch, does it?

Revere rode directly to Lexington and Concord. False. Revere was a key organizer of many riders in an informal, early-warning network (much like a primitive phone tree), and he often carried news from point A to point B for the colonial cause. On April 18, 1775, Revere was first in the chain of many riders who went forth to mobilize the militia and protect colonial munitions stores and leaders from surprise seizure. Fellow rider William Dawes soon joined him, and they later picked up Samuel Prescott.

In Lexington, they warned Samuel Adams and John Hancock that the two were about to be arrested, but the men just thanked them and began arguing about what they should do next. Then the riders headed for Concord, but a regular who was stationed at a checkpoint captured Revere. In the subsequent commotion, Dawes and Prescott escaped— Dawes fell off his horse and decided to call it a night, and Prescott was able to warn Concord.

That's right—Sam Prescott's midnight ride.

Revere fought at Lexington. False. You can't fight while helping another guy lug a chest of documents around town. Revere was close to the fighting, though, with muskets being fired around him. Plus, he was doing more preserving a trunk of secrets than he might have with a musket, especially since the colonial militia broke and ran for it.

Revere has always been considered a national hero. False. He was always a regional hero in Massachusetts, but it was Longfellow's poem that got him into history texts and the memories of schoolkids. The poem overstates Revere's role at the expense of many others', but its mid–Civil War timing was impeccable in capturing public emotion. As often happens, history's heroes can be either forgotten or exaggerated, but they're rarely remembered as they truly were.

QUOTE QUACKERY

When the bewitched women in Shakespeare's Scottish tragedy Macbeth *gathered around the cauldron to summon up a spell or two, they did not dispatch their dirge with the phrase, "Bubble, bubble, toil and trouble."*

No one should ever confuse the musings of quirky quacker Scrooge McDuck with the wise and witty writings of William Shakespeare, but that's exactly what occurred when the peculiar pen of Walt Disney and his stable of scribes met the beautiful balladry of the Bard. In the opening scene of Act 4 of Shakespeare's play *Macbeth*, three witches stand around a steaming kettle and warble the famous phrase, "Double, double, toil and trouble, Fire burn and cauldron bubble." The poetic punch of that couplet remained untainted until we were presented with Disney's classic cartoon "Much Ado About Scrooge," a jocular jaunt that parodies Shakespeare's classic tragedy. In the wonderful world of Disney, the trio of ducks reverses the words in Will's rhyming scheme, declaring, "Bubble, bubble, toil and trouble, Leave this island on the double." From that moment on, things were never the same in Stratford-upon-Avon, as countless schoolchildren were convinced that McDuck's verse was right and the *Macbeth* rhyme was wrong. English teachers around the country could only wring their hands as the Magic Kingdom trumped highbrow culture.

The trend continued into the modern age of television when, in 1991, the comedy series *Home Improvement*, which would later become a number-one-rated program, presented an episode titled, you guessed it, "Bubble, Bubble, Toil and Trouble." The plot revolved around a whirlpool and a botched bathroom renovation. It goes without saying that *Tool Time* in prime time didn't do Shakespeare any favors either.

MARX'S WORD CHOICE

Karl Marx said many things, but he didn't say, "Religion is the opiate of the people."

Opium or opiate? With religious zealots addressing the masses with overblown rhetoric, it's not surprising that secular sensationalists often reference the renowned religious diatribe that Karl Marx authored in February 1843. In the introduction to his paragraph-by-paragraph critique of Hegel's 1820 book *Elements of the Philosophy of Right*, Marx remarked: "Religious suffering is, at one and the same time, the expression of real suffering and a protest against real suffering. Religion is the sigh of the oppressed creature, the heart of a heartless world, and the soul of the soulless conditions. It is the opium of the people."

To some analysts, Marx was saying that religion is a drug that dulls people's pain but leaves them incapable of or unwilling to affect change. To others, the erudite economist was of the opinion that religion provides solace to people in distress and eases whatever pain they may be feeling, much like a drug such as opium. At the time, opium was a legal pain-reducing product, though attempts at its prohibition were beginning to appear.

"SURVIVAL OF THE FITTEST"

This metaphor for natural selection was not coined by Charles Darwin. Its origin can be traced back to the 19th-century economist Herbert Spencer. Yet after Spencer wrote the phrase in *Principles of Biology* (1864), it took on a life of its own.

Spencer conjured the phrase as a reference to Charles Darwin's theory of natural selection, which Spencer had read about upon the 1859 release of *On the Origin of Species by Means of Natural Selection*. Darwin's theory was strictly biological: Given the preconditions of variation, replication, and heritability, traits favorable to a given environment are preserved over time (natural selection), and thus change occurs (evolution). By means of analogy, Spencer brought this concept into the economic realm to describe how the "fittest" societies evolve over time.

Despite popularizing the same phrase, Darwin and Spencer didn't use it in the same way. By "fittest" Darwin did not mean "best" but rather whatever trait allows an organism to survive and reproduce in a given environment, thereby increasing the frequency of said trait. Spencer, on the other hand, did intend fittest to mean "best," and he applied the idea to social evolution, not biology. What Darwin meant by natural selection is best summarized by a quote that actually appeared in *On the Origin of Species*, from the very first edition: "Any variation, however slight . . . if it be in any degree profitable to an individual of any species . . . will tend to the preservation of that individual, and will generally be inherited by its offspring."

ONE GIANT SUCKER

Phineas Taylor Barnum (1810–91) both amused and appalled audiences with his collections of freaks, oddities, and wonders. Writer Herman Melville boldly declared him "sole heir to all . . . lean men, fat women, dwarfs, two-headed cows, amphibious sea-maidens, large-eyed owls, small-eyed mice, rabbit-eating anacondas, bugs, monkies and mummies." In the name of entertainment, he promoted "humbugs"—obvious hoaxes designed to delight and entertain, such as the "Feejee Mermaid" and a woman he claimed was George Washington's 161-year-old nanny.

Barnum insisted that people enjoyed being fooled so long as they got "several times their money's worth." Though it seems likely that such a showman would utter this dismissive phrase, Barnum's acquaintances denied it upon inquiry from his biographer, saying that Barnum treasured and respected his patrons.

START OF THE PUNCHLINE

The true story behind the phrase can be traced to George Hull, a businessman from Binghamton, New York. In 1868, Hull (a fervent atheist) argued with a fundamentalist preacher who insisted the Bible be taken literally, including Genesis 6:4 ("There were giants in the earth in those days"). Hull purchased an enormous slab of gypsum and hired a stonecutter to carve it into a ten-foot-tall statue of a giant with lifelike details such as toenails, fingernails, and pores. The statue was stained with sulfuric acid and ink and shipped to a farm near Cardiff, New York, where it was then buried.

A year later, Hull hired workers to dig a well near the spot where the statue was buried. As he intended, the workers discovered the statue and were excited by their find. (Six months earlier, fossils had been unearthed—with much publicity—at a nearby farm.) Hull had the workers excavate the statue, and then he charged people to see the Cardiff Giant, as it had become known.

Hull sold his statue for nearly $40,000 to a group of exhibitors headed by David Hannum. Barnum became interested in the find and offered to rent it for $50,000, but Hannum refused. Rather than make a higher offer, Barnum built his own Cardiff Giant, which he put on display, declaring that Hannum had sold him the giant after all and that Hannum's was the forgery. Newspapers widely publicized Barnum's story, causing audiences to flock to Barnum while Hannum bitterly declared, "There's a sucker born every minute," in reference to the duped crowds.

CAREFUL WHAT YOU SUE FOR

Hannum sued Barnum for calling his giant a sham. At trial, Hull admitted that the original giant was a hoax. The judge ruled in Barnum's favor, saying that it is not a crime to call a fake a fake.

Afterward, one of Barnum's competitors, Adam Forepaugh, mistakenly attributed (or intentionally misattributed) Hannum's phrase to Barnum. The consummate showman didn't deny saying it; in fact, he thanked Forepaugh for the publicity.

THAT WAS DUMB

> **Apart from hydrogen, the most common thing in the universe is stupidity.**
> —Harlan Ellison

Take solace. In this chapter you'll find lots of precedents for your behavior last weekend.

Yep, people are dumb. In fact, stupidity has to be considered a benchmark of our species across time and culture. There are just too many examples to draw from: putting all your vacation money in slot machines, buying a pet rock, running naked through the outfield at a nationally-televised ballgame . . . you name it, someone is doing it right now. Why? We don't know. Why is there hydrogen? The point is you're not fooling anyone. Boneheaded behavior is embedded in the fabric of your DNA and indeed the universe itself.

SUPREME BUNGLING:
BAD GENERALSHIP IN THE CIVIL WAR

Let's begin this chapter with a look at everyone's favorite oxymoron—military intelligence. The Civil War had more than its share of suicidal attacks, unforgivable lapses in human intelligence, and even cowardice. Some of the generals were admirable leaders who just had bad days; others should never have worn the bars or the stars.

Nathaniel Banks, U.S.A. Banks's many unnecessary losses included Shenandoah Valley and Cedar Mountain (Virginia, 1862), plus Port Hudson (Louisiana, 1863). He didn't get the nickname "Commissary" for his superior logistical skill; rebel troops gave him that nickname in appreciation for the Union provisions they captured from him. His crowning blunder was the Red River Expedition (Louisiana, 1864), in which his troops floundered toward Shreveport without achieving anything.

Braxton Bragg, C.S.A. You would want discipline-stickler Bragg running a basic training center, but not your army. The Bragg cycle would start when he'd botch up in some way: mishandle a battle, or pick the wrong terrain, or fail to exploit a win. His subordinates would either defy him or write home to Richmond begging reprieve. Bragg would learn of this, then punish them for insubordination before committing a new error to restart the process. Eventually, the Confederate government put Bragg to work on the supply-and-draft pipeline, something he was actually good at.

Ambrose Burnside, U.S.A. There's bad, and then there's Burnside's version of bad. His problems began when this competent brigadier gained a second star. Burnside—a modest man—didn't think he had what it took to command the Army of the Potomac, but his superiors felt otherwise. Robert E. Lee spanked Burnside at Fredericksburg (Virginia, 1862), showing that Ambrose's one brilliant command judgment had been that he shouldn't command. Burnside's Homeric error came at Petersburg (Virginia, 1864). Union engineers tunneled beneath Confederate positions and detonated explosives, breaching the lines with a big crater. Burnside sent a force commanded by a drunkard (James Ledlie) into the crater, where they halted long enough for the rebels to contain and mow them down. Burnside's solution: Send more men into the hole to die with the first group! The Battle of the Crater was one of the war's most tragic episodes.

James Ledlie, U.S.A. The charge was GWI (generaling while intoxicated). Ledlie nominally commanded one of the divisions Burnside squandered in the Crater at Petersburg. Instead of leading his men into danger, he stayed behind and got crocked. Drunkenness is one thing in a leader— a number of Civil War generals took a drink—but few deliberately ducked combat. Even incompetent Ambrose Burnside was neither a drunkard nor a coward; Ledlie was both.

Nathan Evans, C.S.A. As drunkards went, Evans had a decent generaling career, except for one incredible blunder at Kinston (North Carolina, 1862). Ordering a fighting withdrawal across a river under heavy Federal assault, Evans burned a bridge behind him. That would have worked well had he not accidentally left half his force on the far bank. Observing the scene from a safe distance, he mistook his forsaken troops' gun smoke for Union fire and ordered his artillery to shell his own men.

Gideon Pillow, C.S.A. This doesn't seem difficult: When you blow a hole in enemy lines, you exploit the hard-won breach. You don't do what Pillow did at Fort Donelson (Tennessee, 1862)—march your guys back to their trenches, giving someone as smart as Ulysses S. Grant time to patch his lines and regroup. While Pillow's 12,000-man garrison hauled down its flag, he fled across the river, thus helping the Union again by avoiding captivity.

David Porter, U.S.A. Admirals, the seagoing version of generals, must also take their medicine. Like Grant, Porter was an outstanding officer who only once opened a jug—but Porter drank the entire thing. In 1865, the Union was trying to capture the tough Fort Fisher (North Carolina). Porter decided that Navy sailors and U.S. Marines armed with swords and pistols could "board" Fort Fisher and capture it, not realizing that the defenders' long-rifled muskets made this a suicidal proposition for the Yankee tars.

HOW MANY IDIOTS OWNED A PET ROCK?

At least 1.3 million by Christmas morning, 1975. And watch who you're calling an idiot!

That figure counts only the original Pet Rocks. In the months before Christmas, thousands of cheaper imitations were also sold, and no one knows how many of those changed hands. Gary Dahl, the marketing genius who thought up the Pet Rock, got the idea from listening to his friends complain about their troublesome pets. He persuaded a former boss to back him financially and arranged to haul two and a half tons of pebbles from Rosarita Beach in Mexico to his Northern California headquarters. After packaging them in carrying crates filled with nesting straw and cut with air holes, he introduced the Pet Rock at gift shows that autumn.

Soon he was shipping thousands of rocks per day to stores such as Neiman-Marcus and Macy's. Dahl earned ninety-five cents for every authentic Pet Rock sold at $3.95. He became a millionaire three weeks before Christmas, appeared on TV talk shows, and was written up in *Newsweek*, *People*, and many major newspapers. Why? What sparked such an insane fad? Dahl took a stab at explaining it, saying, "I think the country was depressed and needed a giggle."

He was probably right, because for most people, the real fun of having a Pet Rock was reading the manual. Written by Dahl and titled *The Care and Training of Your PET ROCK*, the thirty-two-page booklet described how to teach your new pet basic commands such as "Stay," "Sit," and "Play dead." Although rocks learned these tricks quickly, more complicated commands such as "Come" required "extraordinary patience" from the trainer.

Nostalgic attempts to recreate the magic, or take it a step further with Rock Concerts or Rock Families (often with googly eyes glued onto the rocks), fell flat. In 2000, Pet Rocks were packaged and sold with minimal changes to the original design. One noticeable omission in the 2000 version of the manual was the "Attack" command. In 1975, owners were told that when confronted by a mugger, they should, "Reach into your pocket or purse [and] extract your pet rock. Shout the command, ATTACK. And bash the mugger's head in." Presumably, the twenty-first century is too litigious to give this advice to rock owners.

None of the redux sales strategies worked. Pet Rocks enjoyed their fifteen minutes of fame, but after their initial—and legendary—success, all attempts to remarket Pet Rocks have dropped like a stone.

FUMBLING FELONS

KEEP IT TO YOURSELF

A 60-year-old man in Duisburg, Germany, decided to appeal his court conviction for streaking at a girls' soccer match. Perhaps believing it might help his case, the man stripped off all his clothes in the courtroom when the jury adjourned for deliberation. Needless to say, new charges were immediately filed.

DON'T DISPLAY YOUR OWN EVIDENCE

An Italian university student was arrested in 2007 for marijuana charges after dropping his cell phone. Apparently, the student had taken a picture of himself in front of a marijuana plant and then inexplicably used that picture as a screen saver on his phone. That wasn't so bad, until he lost the phone. A retiree found it and turned it over to the police. Upon seeing the picture, police called the student in, where he promptly broke down and confessed to everything, including the location of his crop. He was immediately arrested.

THE INTERNET KNOWS EVERYTHING

Two burglars broke into an indoor amusement center in Colorado Springs, Colorado. Police suspect that they had inside help, as the felons had keys, pass codes, and combinations. What they didn't have, however, was information about the safes—which took them more than 75 minutes to open. Security footage showed them fumbling with the dials. In an attempt to obscure the lens of a security camera, the bungling duo sprayed it with WD-40 lubricant, which cleaned the lens instead. Eventually, one of the burglars left the room. Police later checked a computer in a nearby office and found that the thief had performed Google searches for "how to open a safe" and "how to crack a safe." It must have helped. The two easily opened the safes after that, escaping with cash, a laptop computer, and a PlayStation, totaling more than $12,000.

TAKE YOUR NAME TAG WITH YOU

In June 2007, a man who was admitted to a Newark, New Jersey, hospital was arrested for vandalizing the hospital's helicopter. He apparently left the emergency room and walked onto the helipad. Perhaps searching for drugs, the man entered the helicopter and ransacked it. Damages were estimated around $55,000. The vandal, however, left behind his grocery store name tag in the helicopter. Police swiftly arrested him.

WITCHES EVERYWHERE

In 1692, the quiet little town of Salem Village, Massachusetts, was convulsed in the grip of witchcraft. The only way the town could save itself was to track down every last witch and hang them from the gallows. At least, this seemed to be a good idea to the elders of Salem.

In the early 1690s, Salem Village, a small Massachusetts town on the Danvers River, was beginning to experience growing pains. It was making the rocky transition from farming community to mercantile center; an unpredictable Indian war raged less than 100 miles away; and poor harvests and disease frequently threatened the Puritans who lived there. The community had just weathered a rough winter in early 1692, and as spring finally approached, odd behavior among some of the local children began to frighten the adults.

In February 1692, nine-year-old Betty Parris, the daughter of a local preacher brought in from Boston, began acting bizarrely. She ran about screaming, dove under furniture, contorted in pain, and complained of fever. There was no obvious medical explanation for Betty's condition, but a local minister named Cotton Mather thought he had found one: Betty was a victim of witchcraft. When two of Betty's playmates showed similar symptoms and local medicines failed to cure them, the townspeople drew the only logical conclusion: There was a witch in their midst.

Suspicion first fell on a slave named Tituba, who worked in Betty's home. Tituba had been known to tell the children colorful stories and tales of West Indian voodoo, and when Tituba was caught trying to cure Betty by feeding a "devil cake" to a dog (dogs being common forms of demons), Tituba's guilt seemed assured.

The hunt for Salem's witches took a new turn when the afflicted girls, now seven in all, began accusing other local women of sending evil spirits against them. Tituba and two others were dragged into Ingersoll's Tavern on March 1 and examined by local magistrates. Thoroughly frightened, Tituba confessed to being a witch.

Tituba's confession started a chain of events that would extinguish the lives of 19 men and women before it was all over. Soon, four more women, along with the four-year-old daughter of one of the accused, were collectively accused of practicing witchcraft and sending spirits to torment their accusers. (The young daughter, jailed for eight months, watched as her mother was carted off to the gallows.) The young accusers grew more theatrical in their stories, and during the next several months, they and other witnesses identified some 200 townspeople as witches, all of whom were thrown into the colony's jail.

Panic began to spread. To get a handle on the growing mayhem, Governor William Phips commissioned a seven-judge court to try the accused of witchcraft, a capital offense under Massachusetts law. At Reverend Mather's urging, the court admitted "spectral evidence"—testimony that an accuser had seen the ghostly apparition of a witch—as well as evidence of "witch's teats," moles on a defendant's body on which a familiar spirit, such as a black cat, might suckle.

The judges found the evidence very persuasive, and when one jury failed to convict an accused woman, the court's chief justice, William Stoughton, instructed the jury to go back and reconsider; it then returned with a verdict of guilt.

Armed with this compelling evidence, the court had no choice but to execute the newly discovered witches. Between June 10 and September 22, 19 men and women (one of whom was the village's ex-minister) were carted off to Gallows Hill and hanged. The 80-year-old husband of one witch, who refused to participate in his trial, was punished by pressing, a gruesome execution method in which the sheriff placed large stones on the man's chest until he expired. Four others died in prison, and two dogs were executed as accomplices to witchcraft.

By August, the town's mania began to subside. Better-educated villagers questioned the fantastic evidence against the accused, and in May 1693, Governor Phips shut down the proceedings and freed all remaining defendants. One judge made a public apology for sentencing so many to death, and several jurors admitted that they had been horribly misled by juvenile actors, hysterical townspeople, and fanatical judges.

IF ALL OF ACME'S PRODUCTS BACKFIRE, WHY DOES WILE E. COYOTE KEEP BUYING THEM?

Considering the number of failed ACME armaments, augmentations, and demolition devices that Wile E. Coyote employs in unsuccessful attempts to eradicate the Road Runner, we might conclude that ACME pays the clueless carnivore as a beta tester.

Wile E. Coyote has tried to catch his prospective prey using explosive tennis balls, earthquake pills, do-it-yourself tornado kits, jet-propelled pogo sticks, roller skis, instant icicle makers, and dehydrated boulders. Most of the damage he does is to himself, which makes sense—Wile E. Coyote is an addict.

That's right. In *Chuck Amuck: The Life and Times Of An Animated Cartoonist*, Wile E. Coyote creator Chuck Jones explains: "The Coyote could stop anytime—if he was not a fanatic. Of course he can't quit; he's certain that the next attempt is sure to succeed. He's the personality type that twelve-step programs are made for." Jones's thoughts are right in line with those of the late philosopher George Santayana, who said, "A fanatic is one who redoubles his effort when he has forgotten his aim."

If we want to be more charitable, we might view Wile E. Coyote as a metaphor for the addictive personality. Jones's inspiration for the character came from Mark Twain's description of a wild coyote in the book *Roughing It*. "The cayote [sic] is a living, breathing allegory of Want," Twain wrote. "He is always hungry. He is always poor, out of luck and friendless." Jones always thought of the coyote "as a sort of dissolute collie," he said in a 1989 *New York Times* interview.

So should Wile E. enroll in AA (ACME Anonymous, naturally)? Probably not. As Jones says, "The Coyote is always more humiliated than harmed by his failures." And the embarrassment is never enough to keep him from trying yet another ACME product. So don't quit now, Wile E. One of ACME's devices has to work eventually—right?

RIDICULOUS "FANS ON THE FIELD" MOMENTS

For these misguided fans, "Take Me Out to the Ball Game" could just as easily have turned into "Jailhouse Rock."

TEN-CENT BEER NIGHT

In the planning stages, selling beer for a dime probably seemed like a good promotion back in 1974. But things got a little dicey after approximately 60,000 brews were sold. Fans at Cleveland Municipal Stadium stormed the field as the Indians played the Texas Rangers. Punches were thrown, chairs were used as weapons, and the Rangers were awarded the game.

FLAG-BURNING RESCUE

Chicago Cubs center fielder Rick Monday wasn't amused when a pair of fans ran onto the field at Dodger Stadium on April 25, 1976. He was even less amused when the spectators prepared to set an American flag on fire. Monday swooped in and snatched the flag while police arrested the scofflaws. The stadium gave Monday a standing ovation.

A PITCHER'S DUEL

Fans are accustomed to booing pitchers when they give up key runs. One fan took it to the next level in 1995 after Cubs reliever Randy Myers gave up a home run to give the Houston Astros the lead. The man rushed the pitcher's mound, perhaps to give Myers some advice on what to throw next. Instead, Myers floored him with his forearm.

ATTACKING FANS

Houston right fielder Bill Spiers was on the receiving end of such an attack in 1999 as the team was playing the Milwaukee Brewers. He ended up with a welt under his left eye, a bloody nose, and whiplash. The fan ended up with a beating from pitcher Mike Hampton.

FOOLS AND THEIR MONEY

As Jake wearily feeds quarters into a humming slot machine, a thought occurs to him: "I think this machine is dead. I'd like to try a different one, but I've heard they all have fixed pay cycles. I've been on this one for two hours, so it should be about ready to cough it up. I guess I'll stay put."

The fact is that many such thoughts steer gamblers into repetitive or superstitious habits that have little to no bearing on reality. A modern slot machine just generates numbers. It can't discern between its first spin and its twenty-thousandth, so Jake could easily spend weeks "babysitting" it, hoping for the big payoff. Slot machines do have certain payout percentages, but these are based on millions of spins to reach a jackpot.

Frustrated by its stinginess, Jake finally walks away from his slot machine. An instant later another patron takes Jake's seat, plops in a coin, and hits the super jackpot. If Jake had simply stuck it out, would he be the rich one? Not unless he had pushed the spin button or yanked the handle at precisely the same microsecond as the winner had. The reason is that changes in timing yield completely different results—a phenomenon referred to as the "hero or zero" rule.

Disgusted, Jake decides to rely on another tactic: He'll come back when the place is jam-packed, knowing that more jackpots are won when the casino is crowded. At this point it would be easy to again call Jake a loser, but we won't go there. The reason a casino gives up more jackpots when it's busy is obvious: More people are playing, so more spins are taking place—which means more jackpots will be hit. In the end, Jake might want to stick to scratch-offs.

MOBSTER BOTCHERY

Organized crime is serious business. After all, it usually involves violence, weapons, other people's money, the law, and prison. With those pieces loose on the chessboard, it's really easy to mess things up. Take the two New York mobsters who agreed to do a little job: hit Al Capone. They had a nice trip on the Twentieth Century Limited, but in Chicago they were met at the train, taken someplace quiet, and beaten to death. Pieces of them were sent back with a note: "Don't send boys to do a man's job."

There's also the mistake of not knowing who you're dealing with. Faced with debts in his electrical business, Florida businessperson George Bynum borrowed $50,000 from a mob loan shark. He was able to make $2,500 payments on the interest, but he couldn't pay off the principal, so he decided to go into the crime business himself. He tipped off a burglary gang about a house that he had wired, in exchange for a cut of the take. The burglars broke in, but the home owner was there, and they beat him up. The owner was Anthony "Nino" Gaggi, a Gambino family mobster.

Gaggi found out that Bynum had planned the burglary. On July 13, 1976, John Holland called Bynum from the Ocean Shore Motel and pitched a lucrative wiring contract. When Bynum arrived at the motel, Gaggi and some friends were waiting, and that was the last anyone heard from Bynum.

Often the bungling of criminals is much more humorous. Enrico "Kiko" Frigerio was a Swiss citizen, and when the famed Pizza Connection—a scheme to push heroin through pizza parlors in New York—was broken by the FBI in 1984, he fled to Switzerland. Frigerio stayed there for years, until a documentary film crew decided to do a movie about his life. As technical advisor, he decided to give them a tour of his old New York haunts, but when he stepped off a plane onto U.S. soil, he was immediately arrested. Frigerio hadn't realized that he was still under indictment. Oops!

A CONTINUING COMEDY OF ERRORS

Jimmy Breslin once wrote a comic novel called *The Gang That Couldn't Shoot Straight*. He must have been thinking about New Jersey's DeCavalcante crime family, the only one never given a seat on the Mafia's ruling commission. Vincent "Vinnie Ocean" Palermo ruled the DeCavalcante family like a bad Marx Brothers movie. Once, Palermo's men were given a supply of free cell phones—supplied by the FBI to tap their conversations. Another time, Palermo put a .357 Magnum to the head of a boat mechanic to force him to admit that he'd ruined the motor on Palermo's speedboat. "I was so mad, I bit his nose," Palermo said.

Then there was the time that Palermo and the missus went on vacation, and he decided to hide the family jewelry—$700,000 worth—in the bottom of a trash bag. "My wife took the garbage out for the first time in 20 years, and that was the end of the jewelry." Finally, in 1999, Palermo was arrested and agreed to turn informant in exchange for leniency in sentencing. He helped to put away such stalwarts as Frankie the Beast, Anthony Soft-Shoes, and Frank the Painter. Palermo himself admitted to four murders, including that of newspaper editor Frank Weiss. He said that it was a good career move: "I shot him twice in the head. They made me a captain." He will not be missed.

FROM MIGHTY HUNTER TO MIGHTY IDIOT

In contemporary slang, the term nimrod *is no compliment. It's a word in the same vein as* doofus *and* idiot, *with a hint of jerkdom thrown in for good measure.*

Yet *nimrod* has a considerably prouder history as an *eponym*, or a common noun derived from the name of a person or place. It comes from the biblical figure Nimrod, great-grandson of Noah, who is described in Genesis 10:8 as "a mighty hunter." According to the textual evidence dug up by the *Oxford English Dictionary*, this oblique reference to Nimrod lay dormant for centuries before being lexically resurrected in the sixteenth century.

After a brief incarnation as another word for *tyrant*, it returned to its biblical roots. By the mid-1600s, "skilled hunter" or, more simply, "a person who likes to hunt," had emerged as the primary meaning for *nimrod*.

But how did the word make the semantic jump from mighty hunter to mighty idiot? A widely circulated explanation attributes the shift to none other than cartoon character Bugs Bunny, who in a 1940s cartoon refers to his hapless nemesis, hunter Elmer Fudd, as a "poor little Nimrod." As the explanation goes, cartoon audiences unfamiliar with the biblical reference took this use of *nimrod* not as a nod to Fudd's hunting hobby but as a characterization of his slow-wittedness.

While it's perfectly plausible for a popular cartoon to influence the semantic development of a word in the way that this Looney Tunes tale suggests, there is one problem here. The *OED* dates the earliest use of the dumbed-down *nimrod* to 1933 (in the play *The Great Magoo*)—about a decade before Bugs and Fudd ever crossed paths. Is this evidence completely damning to the theory of cartoon coinage? Perhaps, but don't let that stop you from hunting down another explanation!

WHAT'S THE BEST WAY TO TREAT A HANGOVER?

Indeed, how else to end this chapter? *Veisalgia* is the medical term for your condition. And frankly, the optimal time to treat a wicked hangover is before it even starts, so if your pulse is already pounding in your temples and your stomach is doing back flips, you've missed your best chance to avoid a bad katzenjammer. Still, feel free to read on (if you can bear to keep your eyes open and focused) for some hard-earned advice that can make the morning after that next wild fiasco a little more pleasant.

A great deal of a hangover's agony is caused by simple dehydration. Alcohol is great at sucking the water out of you, so having one glass of water for each cocktail you consume is one of the smartest things that you can do.

Try to remember to drink some more water before you stumble into bed, and put a nice big bottle of H20 on the nightstand to drink when you wake up. Those frequent trips to the bathroom will totally pay off.

Another hint: Stick with alcoholic beverages that are clear. Research shows that transparent tipples like vodka and gin lead to less excruciating hangovers. Why? Darker liquors have more congeners in them. Congeners are by-products of fermentation; as your body processes them, it can produce formaldehyde, which (given formaldehyde's utility as an embalming fluid) helps to explain why you wake up the next morning feeling half dead.

But sometimes, all the foresight in the world won't prevent a world of hangover hurt. So what can you do about it? We recommend a simple course of action: Drink lots of fluids—water, fruit juice, or maybe even a bottle of your favorite sports drink. If you feel extremely dehydrated, avoid coffee and other caffeinated drinks because they'll only dry you out more. Down a pain reliever if you think your stomach can take it (and if your stomach isn't ready yet, you'll probably also want to avoid acidic drinks like orange, grapefruit, and tomato juices).

One of the best things you can do is go back to bed—more sleep will do wonders. If you can't sleep, take a warm shower to improve your circulation and try some bland food like crackers, rice, bananas, or toast. Once you're up, light exercise can help to put the pain behind you. One more thing—and repeat it over and over: "I promise never to drink this much again."

DUMB THINGS PEOPLE HAVE ACTUALLY SAID

"Four. I don't think I could eat eight."
—Yogi Berra, when asked how many pieces his pizza should be sliced into

"[There is] a world market for maybe five computers at most."
—Thomas J. Watson, chairman of IBM, 1943

"I think more people would be alive today if there were a death penalty."
—Nancy Reagan

"With over 50 foreign cars already on sale here, the Japanese auto industry isn't likely to carve out a big slice of the U.S. market."
—Business Week magazine, 1968

"*Not of any commercial value.*"
—Thomas Edison, on the phonograph, 1880

"*Louis Pasteur's theory of germs is ridiculous fiction.*"
—Pierre Pachet, professor of physiology at Toulouse, 1872

"*Ours has been the first, and doubtless to be the last, to visit this profitless locality.*"
—Lt. Joseph Ives, after visiting the Grand Canyon, 1861

"*Aeroplanes are interesting toys but of no military value.*"
—Marshal Ferdinand Foch, French military strategist, 1911

"*A severe depression like that of 1920–1921 is outside the range of probability.*"
—The Harvard Economic Society, 1929

"*Computers in the future may have only 1,000 vacuum tubes and weigh no more than 1.5 tons.*"
—Popular Mechanics Magazine, 1949

"*No matter what happens, the U.S. Navy is not going to be caught napping.*"
—U.S. Secretary of Navy, December 4, 1941

"*Line up alphabetically according to your height.*"
—Casey Stengel

BLAME IT ON THOSE LIZARDS FROM THE STARS

> **When the going gets weird,**
> **the weird turn professional.**
> —Hunter S. Thompson

What's not to love about a cult? Let's say you have
some mystical ideas about invisible entities, vibratory
emanations, and how many wives you can have. Why not
legitimize those ideas? Write an incoherent manifesto, gain
a following, and go off and practice akashic conspirituality
in the woods?

Thanks to our First Amendment rights, this is a great
country in which to do just that—unhindered by anything
except a little social censure or a lingering sense of
reality. You're free to believe that alien reptiles direct your
thoughts or that the Time of Doom begins next Thursday.
Judging from history, there will always be a weird minority
wanting to do just that.

CRAZY CULTS AND UNBELIEVABLE BELIEFS

THE MILLERITES

William Miller, a farmer in northern New York, founded a doomsday cult in the 1800s. Studying the Bible convinced Miller that humanity was due for damnation. He began preaching this message in the early 1830s. His first prediction was that Jesus Christ would "come again to the earth, cleanse, purify and take possession of the same" between March 1843 and March 1844. When a comet appeared early in 1843, a number of his followers killed themselves, believing the end was near. However, when his prophecy didn't come to pass and the world survived, Miller stood by his message but became reluctant to set actual dates. Some of his followers took it upon themselves to announce October 22, 1844, as the big day, and Miller reluctantly agreed. This date came to be known as The Great Disappointment. Regardless, Miller and his followers established a basis on which the Seventh-Day Adventist Church was later founded.

THE RAELIAN MOVEMENT

A belief in unidentified flying objects has haunted humanity for generations, with thousands claiming to have had direct contact with alien beings from other worlds. Claude Vorilhon, a French race car driver and one-time musician, asserted that he was visited by an extraterrestrial in 1973. It was a life-altering experience for him that caused him to change his name to Rael and found the Raelian Church. Rael's religion proclaims that the Elohim ("those who came from the sky") created everything on Earth. Although many turn a skeptical eye toward Vorilhon, whose faith also preaches free love, the Raelian Movement is said to include as many as 65,000 members worldwide.

THE VAMPIRE CHURCH

With offices located throughout the United States, Canada, and Australia, the Vampire Church provides the initiated and the curious with an opportunity to learn more about vampirism. However, don't expect to find much about the "undead," as vampires have been portrayed in stories since Bram Stoker wrote *Dracula* in 1897. Instead, the church offers insight into vampirism as a physical condition that sometimes requires unusual energy resources, such as blood. In addition, it explains the difference between psychic vampires and elemental vampires. According to the church's Web site, "The Vampire Church continues to grow as more true vampires find the haven they so seek with others of this condition and the knowledge and experience of others here."

THE CHURCH OF EUTHANASIA

"Save the Planet—Kill Yourself." These words are the battle cry of the Church of Euthanasia, which was established by Boston resident Chris Korda in 1992. Korda, a musician, had a dream one night about an alien who warned her that Earth was in serious danger. The extraterrestrial, which Korda dubbed "The Being," stressed the importance of protecting the planet's environment through population control. As a result of the encounter, Korda established the Church of Euthanasia, which supports suicide, abortion, and sodomy (defined as any sex act that is not intended for procreation). According to the church's Web site, members are vegetarian, but they "support cannibalism for those who insist on eating flesh." Although it reportedly has only about 100 members in the Boston area, the church claims that thousands worldwide have visited its Web site and been exposed to its message.

BRANCH DAVIDIANS

Followers of David Koresh looked upon him as one of God's messengers. Koresh thought of himself the same way. The U.S. government, however, had a different point of view (including allegations of polygamy, child abuse, and rape). Koresh and many followers of his religious sect were killed in 1993 when federal agents attempted to raid the group's compound near Waco, Texas. The ensuing 51-day standoff ended on April 19 when the Branch Davidian compound burned to the ground. The fallout wasn't limited to Koresh and company—the federal government was highly criticized for its handling of the situation.

MANSON FAMILY

More than 40 years after his followers murdered Leno and Rosemary LaBianca and actress Sharon Tate, the name "Charles Manson" still sends a chill down the spines of many people. Manson was charged with murder and conspiracy and has been serving a life sentence. Among the members of the Manson family was Lynette "Squeaky" Fromme, who attempted to assassinate President Gerald R. Ford in 1975.

HEAVEN'S GATE

UFOs and Comet Hale-Bopp were the basis of this cult, which was led by Marshall Applewhite. Members believed that Earth was about to be "recycled" and instead opted to commit mass suicide. Thirty-nine members of the cult (including Applewhite as well as the brother of *Star Trek* actress Nichelle Nichols) were found dead in a San Diego mansion in 1997.

ORDER OF THE SOLAR TEMPLE

Cultists do like their space-aged names . . . even secret societies headquartered in Europe. Started in 1984 and based on the ideals of the Knights Templar, leaders sought to unify many different beliefs before the end of the world. Things went bad for the members in 1994 after one of its founders, Joseph Di Mambro, ordered the murder of the three-month-old child of another member. The reason? The child was the antichrist (at least according to Di Mambro). A few days later, members in Canada and Switzerland are believed to have killed other followers before committing suicide.

THE PEOPLE'S TEMPLE

About 900 followers of a quasi-religious group led by Reverend Jim Jones drank cyanide as part of a mass suicide in Jonestown, Guyana, in 1978. Many experts view the event as one of the largest mass suicides in recorded history. For the record, Jones chose not to imbibe of the poisonous drink he offered the others. He shot himself in the head instead. Oh, but the story isn't over. Before things fell apart at his headquarters, Jones ordered a group of his followers to a nearby Georgetown airstrip to stop the departure of some People's Temple followers who had lost the faith. The armed men opened fire on the group as they were departing. Among those killed was U.S. Representative Leo Ryan of California, who had traveled to Guyana to investigate the cult on the behalf of concerned family members.

ONE REPTILE TO RULE THEM ALL

Some people are ruled by their pets; others are ruled by their work. Conspiracy theorist David Icke believes that we're all being ruled by reptilian humanoids.

WORLDWIDE DOMINATION

David Icke has worn many hats: journalist, news anchor for the BBC, spokesman for the British Green Party, and professional soccer player. But after a spiritual experience in Peru in 1991, he took on another role: famed conspiracy theorist.

Like many other conspiracy theorists, Icke believes that a group called the Illuminati, or "global elite," controls the world. According to these theorists, the group manipulates the economy and uses mind control to usher humanity into a submissive state. Icke also believes that the group is responsible for organizing such tragedies as the Holocaust and the Oklahoma City bombings.

Some of the most powerful people in the world are members, claims Icke, including ex-British Prime Minister Tony Blair and former U.S. President George H. W. Bush, as well as leaders of financial institutions and major media outlets. However, not all members are human. According to Icke, those at the top of the Illuminati bloodlines are vehicles for a reptilian entity from the constellation Draco. These shape-shifters can change from human to reptile and back again, and they are essentially controlling humanity.

ONTO SOMETHING OR ON SOMETHING?

In the documentary *David Icke: Was He Right?*, Icke claims that many of his earlier predictions, including a hurricane in New Orleans and a "major attack on a large city" between the years 2000 and 2002, have come true. But are we really being ruled by reptilian humanoids or is Icke's theory a bunch of snake oil? Icke was nearly laughed off the stage in a 1991 appearance on a BBC talk show. But with 16 published books, thousands attending his speaking engagements, and thousands of weekly hits to his Web site, perhaps it's Icke who's having the last laugh.

THE ONEIDA COMMUNITY

Think the 1960s were a wacky time for religious cults in America? The mid-1800s has a surprise for boomers. Perhaps the most successful "utopian community" was the Oneida Community of upstate New York.

JOHN H. NOYES

A Vermonter, Noyes was born in 1811. In the 1830s, while studying divinity at Yale, he decided a Christian could transcend sin. He called this philosophy *Perfectionism*. When Noyes pronounced himself without sin, Yale cast the first stone by revoking his ministry license and kicking him out.

PUTNEY

Noyes yearned to build a Perfectionist community. After a spiritual crisis (or perhaps a bout of psychological self-torment), which he considered a desperate Satanic assault, he moved back to Putney, Vermont, where his family lived.

Converting his siblings and some locals, he insisted Christ's second coming had already occurred. According to Noyes, marriage and monogamy were nonexistent in Heaven—but sex wasn't. (Noyes himself got married, notwithstanding.) For the next nine years, he gathered and taught his flock.

Members spent their time farming, studying Scripture, and publishing a magazine. Women shared ownership and benefits with relative equality. As for sex, Noyes taught a doctrine called "complex marriage" (all males are married to all females). Men, he taught, should practice "male continence"—refraining from ejaculation unless children were desired. It was the best sexual deal American women would see until the 1960s.

Here began Noyes's concept of "Bible Communism": communally held property, focused on biblical teachings (as interpreted by Noyes). Group criticism sessions were a social norm. But remember: Sino-Soviet Communism hadn't been invented, nor had Lenin, gulags, Mao, etc. Marx only wrote the *Communist Manifesto* in 1848, just as Noyes's community was moving to New York. Noyes would have considered Marx proof of Satan's ability to pervert Scripture.

The Putney situation finally imploded in 1847, when the local sheriff arrested Noyes for adultery. Compelled to flee Vermont, in 1848 Noyes found his people's Zion: 40 acres and a sawmill owned by some Perfectionists near Oneida, New York. By year-end, the Oneida Community was 87 strong and busy as beavers: buying and clearing land, planting, building.

Many new arrivals brought useful skills. Noyes believed people should change jobs often to ward off drudgery. Complex marriage meant that postmenopausal women initiated boys into sex after puberty, until the males learned control. Older men (often Noyes himself) initiated girls into sex shortly after menarche.

In practice, Noyes decided who should have sex, prioritizing his own very healthy appetites in this regard. Since God advised Noyes, disagreeing with Noyes equaled disagreement with God. Those who disagreed with God/Noyes were welcome to hit the bricks.

The community invested and thrived, growing to about 300 members. Oneida women invented bloomeresque pantaloons two years before Amelia Bloomer. Industries arose: canning, silk, animal traps, furniture, and eventually silverware. Oneida hired outside employees, treating them well.

DOWNFALL

By 1879, the Oneida experiment was a great commercial success but socially beleaguered. Noyes's attempt to install his son as his successor hadn't set well. Dissidents wanted to abandon complex marriage. When Noyes learned of his impending arrest for statutory rape, he bailed to Canada, where he advised his members from afar.

The remaining members reorganized Oneida as a joint stock company and kept up the business. The firm sold off all but the silverware business by 1916. In 2005, Oneida Limited finally outsourced silverware manufacture overseas. The last member of the community died in 1950.

THE NAZCA MYSTERY

When in doubt about the purpose of something from an ancient culture, why not devise lurid theories about space aliens?

Flying above the rocky plains northwest of Nazca, Peru, in 1927, aviator Toribio Mejía Xesspe was surprised to see gigantic eyes looking up at him. Then the pilot noticed that the orbs stared out of a bulbous head upon a cartoonish line drawing of a man, etched over hundreds of square feet of the landscape below.

The huge drawing—later called "owl man" for its staring eyes—turned out to be just one of scores of huge, 2,000-year-old images scratched into the earth over almost 200 square miles of the parched Peruvian landscape.

There is a 360-foot-long monkey with a whimsically spiraled tail, along with a 150-foot-long spider, and a 935-foot pelican. Other figures range from hummingbird to killer whale. Unless the viewer knows what to look for, they're almost invisible from ground level. There are also geometric shapes and straight lines that stretch for miles across the stony ground.

SO IT MUST HAVE BEEN DONE BY ANCIENT ASTRONAUTS, RIGHT?

The drawings have been dated to a period between 200 BC and AD 600. Obviously, there were no airplanes from which to view them back then. So why were they made? And for whose benefit?

In his 1968 book *Chariots of the Gods?*, the controversial Swiss author Erich Von Däniken popularized the idea that the drawings and lines were landing signals and runways for starships that visited this barren patch of southern Peru long before the modern era. In his interpretation, the owl man is instead an astronaut in a helmet. Von Däniken's theory caught on among UFO enthusiasts. Many science-fiction novels and films make reference to this desert in Peru's Pampa Colorado region as a site with special significance to space travelers.

COMING DOWN TO EARTH

Examined up close, the drawings consist of cleared paths—areas where someone removed reddish surface rocks to expose the soft soil beneath. In the stable desert climate—averaging less than an inch of rain per year—the paths have survived through many centuries largely intact.

Scientists believe the Nazca culture—a civilization that came before the Incas—drew the lines. The style of the artwork is similar to that featured on Nazca pottery. German-born researcher Maria Reiche (1903–1998) showed how the Nazca could have laid out the figures using simple surveying tools such as ropes and posts.

In the 1980s, American researcher Joe Nickell duplicated one of the drawings, a condor, showing that the Nazca could have rendered parts of the figures "freehand"—that is, without special tools or even scale models. Nickell also demonstrated that despite their great size, the figures can be identified as drawings even from ground level. No alien technology would have been required to make them.

MYSTERIOUS NONETHELESS

As for why the Nazca drew their giant doodles across an uninhabitable desert, no one is sure. Reiche noted that some of the lines may have astronomical relevance. For example, one seems to point to where the sun sets at the winter solstice. Some lines may also have pointed toward possible underground water sources—crucially important information to desert people.

Most scholars think that the marks were part of the Nazca religion. They may have been footpaths followed during ritual processions. And although it's extremely unlikely that they were intended for extraterrestrials, many experts think it likely that the lines were oriented toward Nazca gods—perhaps a monkey god, a spider god, and so on, who could be imagined gazing down from the heavens upon likenesses of themselves.

THE HOUSE OF DAVID

Members of the House of David religious community didn't know exactly when Jesus Christ would return to Earth, but they were certain of the where—Benton Harbor, Michigan.

While they waited for Christ's return, they built a settlement, erected a roller coaster, and followed the biblical vow of the Nazirites to never cut their hair.

THE BEGINNINGS

The House of David's beliefs were rooted in the teachings of Joanna Southcutt (1750–1814). She believed that she was the first of seven angelic messengers who would usher in the millennium (Revelation 10:7).

Like other millennialists, she professed that Christ would reign on Earth during a thousand-year period of peace. Gathered with him would be the elect—the 144,000 descendants of the scattered tribes of Israel.

In 1903, Kentucky-born Benjamin Purnell (1861–1927) started the House of David commune. Trusting in a divine inspiration, his wife, Mary, believed the 144,000 Christian-Israelites would gather in Benton Harbor to await Christ's arrival. With pamphlets and a 780-page book (*The Star of Bethlehem, The Living Roll of Life*), the Purnells attracted followers from the United States, England, and Australia.

The open invitation to join the House of David was hard for some to resist. Although the followers were required to sell their belongings and give the proceeds to the House of David, this was considered a small, temporary sacrifice relative to what they expected to receive in return. After all, they would be among the 144,000 who would rule with Christ on Earth and would accompany Christ to heaven, where they would rank higher than the angels.

By the end of 1903, more than 300 people had joined the House of David, fully trusting in the authority of the Purnells. The group purchased property, shared living quarters, generated electricity, grew their own food, and became vegetarians (a diet they deemed appropriate for the Garden of Eden). Members also took a vow of celibacy.

ENTERTAINMENT

While members of the House of David were patiently waiting for the millennium, they turned to business to keep them busy. In 1908, the Purnells opened Eden Springs, an amusement park with a giant roller coaster, miniature trains, and a zoo with lions, bears, and wandering peacocks. Eden Springs also featured a baseball field, a bowling alley, silent movies, and a variety of musical entertainment, including a band that once performed under John Philip Sousa. In the 1920s, as many as 200,000 nonmembers visited the park each summer.

Baseball also became important. Around 1915, ballplayers from the House of David formed a traveling team that barnstormed across the country. Playing with long hair and beards (they were forbidden to cut their hair), they generated income and gathered converts.

TROUBLE IN EDEN

The Benton Harbor settlement may have looked like Eden on its surface, but scandal lurked. While some lived in luxury, others were allegedly given no more than turnips and carrots to eat. Meanwhile, leaders ignored their vows of celibacy.

Beginning as early as 1907, Purnell was accused of business fraud, sexual indiscretion, and rape, but it took years for the accusations and evidence to support a conviction. In 1927, the state of Michigan brought Purnell to court. Armed with 225 witnesses, 75 depositions, and 15,000 pages of recorded testimony, attorneys were certain Purnell would face time behind bars. However, he died in 1929 before he could be sentenced. The House of David divided.

In 1930, 218 members followed H.T. Dewhirst, the board director. The settlement flourished—though he turned the preaching auditorium into a beer garden. Meanwhile, Mary Purnell led 217 followers to a new location—just two blocks from the original House of David. She reorganized the group, calling it "Mary's City of David."

BASEBALL PREVAILS

Though neither of the new settlements garnered the popularity of the original community, both groups fielded successful baseball teams for the next two decades. (They both used the name "House of David.") They recruited some nonmembers to play, but they were still required to wear long hair and whiskers. Games often boasted trumpets, donkeys, and the immensely popular "pepper game." During the fifth inning, three players stood on the mound, performing sideways tosses, fake throws, and behind-the-back moves before they actually threw the ball to the catcher.

Despite their carnival antics, the House of David teams were highly skilled, defeating 75 percent of their opponents. In 1933, a House of David team faced the Cardinals at Sportsman's Park in St. Louis. Led by female southpaw Jackie Mitchell, the House of David won, 8–6. (Mitchell was not required to wear a fake beard.)

THE COLOR BARRIER

The House of David teams also played against Negro League teams, including the Kansas City Monarchs, and used their immense popularity to help erode the color barrier. According to some reports, the House of David team wouldn't play the local team unless the locals played a Negro League team first.

THE INTERGALACTIC JOURNEY OF SCIENTOLOGY

There are few who don't know about the aura of mystery and scandal that surrounds the Church of Scientology, which boasts a small membership and a seismic pocketbook. Scientology frequently graces the headlines, with stories ranging from accounts of Tom Cruise tomfoolery to an endless stream of lawsuits and accusations of bribery and abuse.

The fantastical elements to the saga of Scientology were perhaps written into the religion from its beginning, given that Scientology sprang from the fertile mind of its late creator, pulp fiction writer turned religious messiah, L. Ron Hubbard. Born in 1911, Hubbard began his writing career in the 1930s after flunking out of college. Hubbard had always preferred imagination to reality: Accounts of his past reveal hallucinogenic drug abuse and an obsession with black magic and Satanism. In between prolific bouts of writing, Hubbard served in the Navy during World War II, became involved in various start-up ventures, and, of course, dabbled in black magic ceremonies. Allegation has it that Hubbard and wealthy scientist friend John Parsons performed a ritual in which they attempted to impregnate a woman with the antichrist. The woman was Parsons's girlfriend, but she soon became Hubbard's second wife—though he was still married to his first wife.

DOWN TO A SCIENCE

In 1949, Hubbard developed a self-help process that he called Dianetics. Humanity's problems, according to Dianetics, stem from traumas of past lives. These traumas are called *engrams*, and Hubbard's own e-meter (a machine using simple lie detector technology) can identify and help eliminate them. Getting rid of engrams can have amazing results—from increasing intelligence to curing blindness. The first Dianetics article appeared in a sci-fi publication called *Astounding Science Fiction*. In 1950, Hubbard opened the Hubbard Dianetic Research Foundation in New Jersey, and in that same year *Dianetics: The Modern Science of Mental Health* was published and sold well.

Hubbard and his followers attempted to establish Dianetics as an official science. But the medical profession didn't appreciate Dianetics masquerading as science. The Dianetic Research Foundation came under investigation by the IRS and the American Medical Association. Hubbard closed his clinics and fled New Jersey.

ACTUALLY, IT'S A RELIGION . . .

Dianetics wasn't making the cut as a scientific theory, so Hubbard played another card. Years before, Hubbard is reputed to have told a friend "writing for a penny a word is ridiculous. If a man really wants to make a million dollars, the best way would be to start his own religion." After fleeing Jersey, Hubbard moved to Phoenix, Arizona, declared Dianetics an "applied religious philosophy," and, in 1954, Hubbard's organization was recognized as a religion by the IRS and granted tax-exempt status.

Thus the Church of Scientology was born. Hubbard added new stories to the original Dianetics creation, and by the 1960s, humans were spiritual descendants of the alien Thetans, who were banished to live on Earth by the intergalactic terrorist dictator Xenu 75 million years ago. Scientologist disciples must not only expel the traumas of past lives but of past lives on different planets. Discovering these traumas is an expensive process, so the Church actively recruits wealthy devotees. As for Hubbard, he died in 1986, soon after the IRS accused him of stealing $200 million from the Church. Today, Scientology and its various offshoot nonprofit groups and private business ventures continue to hold a vast fortune, and Scientology's ongoing litigation with the IRS, the press, and ex-devotees (hundreds of lawsuits are pending) are so bizarre, they seem almost out of this world.

AMERICA'S ISLAND KING

Few people would believe that a separate empire with its own full-fledged king once existed within the borders of the United States of America. But James Jesse Strang was indeed crowned ruler of a Lake Michigan island kingdom in the mid-1800s. His bizarre road to royalty, though, began in southeastern Wisconsin.

GROWING THE GARDEN

Strang was born in 1813 in Scipio, New York. He moved to Wisconsin in 1843 with his wife, Mary, to a large parcel of land just west of what would become the city of Burlington.

Strang set up a law practice and, thanks to family connections, met the Mormon prophet Joseph Smith on a trip to Nauvoo, Illinois. Strang's rise to fame began, as Smith immediately appointed him an elder in the faith and authorized him to start a Mormon "stake" in Wisconsin named Voree, which meant "Garden of Peace."

Mormons from around the country flocked to Voree to build homes on the rolling, forested tract along the White River. A few months after Strang became a Mormon, Joseph Smith was killed. To everyone's amazement, Strang produced a letter that appeared to have been written and signed by Joseph Smith, which named Strang as the church's next Prophet.

Another leader named Brigham Young, whom you may have heard of, also claimed that title, and Young eventually won. As a result, Strang broke away to form his own branch.

SECRETS FROM THE SOIL

In September 1845, Strang made a stunning announcement. He said that a divine revelation had told him to dig under an oak tree in Voree located on a low rise called the "Hill of Promise." Four followers armed with shovels dug under the tree and unearthed a box containing some small brass plates, each only a few inches tall.

The plates were covered with hieroglyphics, crude drawings of the White River settlement area, and a vaguely Native American human figure holding a scepter. Strang said he was able to translate them using special stones, like the ones Joseph Smith had used to translate similar buried plates in New York. The writing, Strang said, was from a lost tribe of Israel that had somehow made it to North America. He managed to show the plates to hundreds of people before they mysteriously disappeared.

As his number of followers grew, he created sub-groups among them. There was the commune-style Order of Enoch, and the secretive Illuminati, who pledged their allegiance to Strang as "sovereign Lord and King on earth." Infighting developed within the ranks, and area non-Mormons also raised objections to the community. Some Burlington residents even went so far as to try to persuade wagonloads of Voree-bound emigrants not to join Strang.

In 1849, Strang received a second set of divine messages, called the Plates of Laban. He said they had originally been carried in the Ark of the Covenant. They contained instructions called *The Book of the Law of the Lord*, which Strang again translated with his helpful stones. The plates were not shown to the group at that time, but they did eventually yield support, some would say rather conveniently, for the controversial practice of polygamy.

POLYGAMY PROBLEMS

Strang had a personal reason for getting divine approval to have multiple wives. In July 1849, a 19-year-old woman named Elvira Field secretly became Strang's second wife. There was just one little problem—he hadn't divorced his first one. Soon, Field was traveling with him posing as a young man named Charlie Douglas, with her hair cut short and wearing a man's black suit. Yet, the "clever" disguise did little to hide Field's ample figure.

At about that time, Strang claimed another angel visited to tell him it was time to get out of Voree. Strang was to lead his people to a land surrounded by water and covered in timber. This land, according to Strang, was Beaver Island, the largest of a group of islands in the Beaver Archipelago north of Charlevoix, Michigan. It had recently been opened to settlement, and the Strangites moved there in the late 1840s.

THE PROMISED ISLAND

On July 8, 1950, Strang donned a crown and red cape as his followers officially dubbed him King of Beaver Island. Falling short of becoming King of the United States, he was later elected to Michigan's state legislature, thanks to strong voter turnout among his followers. Perhaps reveling in his new power, eventually, he took three more young wives, for a total of five.

On the island, Strang's divine revelations dictated every aspect of daily life. He mandated that women wear bloomers and that their skirts measure a certain length, required severe lashings for adultery, and forbade cigarettes and alcohol. Under this strict rule, some followers began to rebel. In addition, relations with local fishermen soured as the colony's businesses prospered.

On June 16, 1856, a colony member named Thomas Bedford, who had previously been publicly whipped, recruited an accomplice and then shot Strang. The king survived for several weeks and was taken back to Voree by his young wives. He died in his parents' stone house—which still stands near Mormon Road on State Highway 11. At the time, all four of his young wives were pregnant. And back in Michigan, it wasn't long before local enemies and mobs of vigilantes from the mainland forcibly removed his followers from Beaver Island.

James Jesse Strang was buried in Voree, but his remains were later moved to a cemetery in Burlington. A marker, which has a map of the old community, stands just south of Highway 11 where it crosses the White River, and several of the old cobblestone houses used by group members are preserved and bear historical markers. Strang's memory also lives on in a religious group formed by several of his followers, the Reorganized Church of Jesus Christ of Latter-Day Saints.

YOUR DUMB QUESTIONS, ANSWERED DISCREETLY

Get your facts first, and then you can distort 'em as much as you please.
—Mark Twain

This scrap of wry wit does much to explain Twain's trajectory from suspect journalist to great American storyteller. It also serves notice to the rest of us: when in doubt, verify your source.

In this chapter we examine some of those curious maxims and theories you've been hearing for years at the office, church bingo, and by crazy uncles—and provide some fact-based counterpunches to knock the wind out of the windbags. Rest assured, you won't go into a tailspin of confusion the next time you're at the water cooler and the conversation turns to the accuracy of the Farmer's Almanac, whether coffee stunts your growth, or why animals don't need glasses. You're welcome.

WILL COFFEE STUNT YOUR GROWTH?

This is one of the many white lies that your mother told you. Don't be mad at her, though—she was only thinking of your health. And in an indirect way, she was right. Nutritionists recommend that growing children keep away from super-caffeinated drinks, coffee included. But it's not because these concoctions affect a child's height—research shows coffee has zero impact on growth.

At one time, coffee was believed to cause osteoporosis, a disease that decreases bone density and can result in fractures and breaks. Fractures of the spine can have horrible consequences, including back pain, deformity, and loss of height. Hence, your mother's concern that coffee would stunt your growth.

But the connection between caffeine and osteoporosis was ultimately debunked. Bone expert Robert P. Heaney concluded from his studies that research linking coffee and osteoporosis had been focused on the elderly, many of whom had replaced milk and other calcium-rich drinks with coffee. In doing so, these people were cutting out a source of nutrition and doing nothing to compensate for the subsequent lack of calcium.

Just one glass of milk per day can make up for this calcium deficiency, according to a 1988–1991 study of 980 women in Rancho Bernardo, California. The women, ages fifty to ninety-eight, underwent bone-density tests for the duration of the study. Part of the study included a self-reported list of foods and drinks that each woman consumed in a day. The results showed that bone density was indeed decreased in women who drank at least two cups of coffee each day; however, such a change was not seen in women who offset their coffee intake by drinking at least one glass of milk per day.

But back to kids. They can drink coffee without worrying about stunting their growth, but there might be other problems involved. High doses of caffeine throughout the day can lead to anxiety and jitteriness, and can also affect sleep patterns. For kids, especially those who have a hard time sitting still in the first place, too much caffeine can make it difficult to concentrate in school. Moderation is the key. A soda or a cup of coffee here and there won't hurt you. It might make you irritable and shaky, but it won't make you short.

WILL LISTENING TO MOZART MAKE MY BABY SMARTER?

That depends on your definition of smarter. When researchers in a 1993 study had participants listen to a Mozart sonata, they found that those people scored slightly higher on spatial-reasoning tests for about ten or fifteen minutes. That's what the researchers tested, that's all they claimed, and their methods seemed sound.

But within a year, the *New York Times* wrote an article in which it summarized, cheekily, that "listening to Mozart actually makes you smarter," and we were off to the races. In 1997, Don Campbell published a book called *The Mozart Effect: Tapping the Power of Music to Heal the Body, Strengthen the Mind, and Unlock the Creative Spirit*. Then came Campbell's *The Mozart Effect for Children*. If the *New York Times* piece showed the suggestive power of the media, Campbell's books demonstrated the power of parental love. Here was a chance for a new generation of über-parents to achieve several desirable things simultaneously: They could help their kids become smarter, give them culture, and assuage their own residual guilt for having listened to Iron Maiden when they were young and impressionable.

Few separate studies have corroborated the limited findings of the original research. Other researchers have argued that Mozart doesn't make listeners smarter—it simply puts them in a better mood, which can translate to temporarily better scores on certain kinds of tests. Mozart's music also has been shown to cause significant—though again temporary—decreases in brain activity that leads to epileptic seizures.

In other words, there is little doubt that Mozart's music—considered to be both abstractly complex and aurally ingratiating—has a fleeting positive effect on people. But does this mean you are smarter for listening? And is it just Mozart? A composition by the Greek composer Yanni—whose cheesy fare you might know from infomercials—has been shown to have similar effects.

You'll have trouble finding many scientists who say Mozart makes anyone smarter. "Enjoyment arousal" is what one scientist calls it. That's certainly a good thing, but it's not enough to guarantee your children will go to Harvard—or will even prefer Mozart to their generation's version of Iron Maiden.

ARE THERE REALLY ONLY "SIX DEGREES" SEPARATING YOU FROM ANY OTHER PERSON?

The idea isn't as far-fetched as you might think. The "six degrees" theory holds that through no more than five mutual acquaintances, you can reach anybody on the planet. For example, you might get to the Queen of England because your cousin did time with a roadie who toured with Paul McCartney, who's tight with the Queen because she knighted him.

The notion first popped up in a 1929 book of short stories by Hungarian writer Frigyes Karinthy. In one story, a character suggests that he could connect to anybody with no more than five people between them. In 1967, a Harvard professor named Stanley Milgram put this notion to the test. He sent letters to several hundred randomly selected people in Kansas and Nebraska, giving each person the name and basic description of someone in Massachusetts. Each participant was supposed to send the letter to an acquaintance who might be closer to the final target; all of the participants along the chain mailed postcards back to Harvard to signal that they had passed on the letter. One letter got to the target in only two steps, though others took almost a dozen steps; Milgram claimed that the median was 5.5 steps. John Guare referenced the idea in his 1990 play *Six Degrees of Separation* (which was made into a movie in 1993), and the term became famous.

Two Cornell researchers were inspired to attack the question mathematically. In a study published in 1998, they explained the fundamental qualities of a "small-world" network. If you picture the human social network graphically, with people as points and relationships as lines between the points, you naturally get ordered clusters of interconnected dots—a lot of the people in your social circle and residential area know each other or are only one mutual acquaintance away from each other. This is an *ordered* network. But there is an element of randomness—the odd connection to someone who's well outside the cluster. This is a *disordered* network. The researchers found that if a small percentage of connections in a mostly ordered network are random—that is, connections between points that go outside ordered clusters—you create shortcuts all over the network. This can make any individual point only a small number of connections away from any other.

For example, if you've always lived in Detroit, most of your friends probably live in Motown, too. Collectively, you form a cluster of many interconnected people. But let's say that your cousin's college roommate lives in Mumbai, India. Through that link, you're connected to a cluster of people in India, and—through you—so is everyone you know in Detroit. And since all of these people have their own random connections, you end up being linked to clusters all over the world.

According to the researcher's model, if only 1 percent of all connections in a network are this sort of random leap between clusters, any two points (e.g., people) end up being closely connected. This is the same basic phenomenon that connects the hundred billion neurons in your brain. This study, and others like it, shows that there might indeed be only six degrees separating you from any other person. Find the right connections, and you'll be enjoying high tea with the Queen.

WHY DON'T ANIMALS NEED GLASSES?

Humans are so quick to jump to conclusions. Just because you've never sat next to an orangutan at the optometrist's office or seen a cat adjust its contact lenses, you assume that animals don't need corrective eyewear.

Animals do develop myopia (nearsightedness), though it seems less widespread in nature than among humans. For one thing, nearsighted animals—especially carnivores—would have an extremely difficult time hunting in the wild. As dictated by the rules of natural selection, animals carrying the myopia gene would die out and, thus, wouldn't pass on the defective gene.

For years, nearsightedness was thought to be mainly hereditary, but relatively recent studies have shown that other factors may also contribute to the development of myopia. Some researchers have suggested that myopia is rare in illiterate societies and that it increases as societies become more educated. This doesn't mean that education causes nearsightedness, but some scientists have speculated that reading and other "close work" can play a role in the development of the condition.

In accordance with this theory, a study of the Inuit in Barrow, Alaska, conducted in the 1960s found that myopia was much more common in younger people than in older generations, perhaps coinciding with the introduction of schooling and mass literacy in Inuit culture that had recently occurred. But schooling was just one component of a larger shift—from the harsh, traditional lifestyle of hunting and fishing at the edge of the world to a more modern, Western lifestyle. Some scientists believe that the increase of myopia was actually due to other changes that went along with this shift, such as the switch from eating primarily fish and seal meat to a more Western diet. This diet is heavier on processed grains, which, some experts believe, can have a bad influence on eye development.

And this brings us back to animals. Your beloved Fido subsists on ready-made kibble that's heavy on processed grains, but its ancient ancestors ate raw flesh. If this switch to processed grains might have a negative effect on the eyesight of humans, why not in animals, too?

Unfortunately, there's not much we can do for a nearsighted animal. Corrective lenses are impractical, glasses would fall off, and laser surgery is just too darn expensive. Sorry, Fido.

DO PEOPLE REALLY USE ONLY 10 PERCENT OF THEIR BRAINS?

While it may seem like your coworkers aren't giving their all, synaptically speaking, it's not true that 90 percent of the brain goes unused. Even a day spent popping Bubble Wrap and watching Barney and Friends puts your gray matter to work.

This doesn't mean that all your circuits are firing at once, though. Different parts of the brain are dedicated to different tasks—the occipital lobes in the back of your brain handle visual information, for example—so depending on what you're doing, you may not be using everything at any particular moment. But scans of brain activity show that people use the whole enchilada over the course of a typical day.

It's not clear where the "10 percent" notion came from, but it likely stemmed from the fact that for a long time, scientists had no idea how the brain works. They were especially clueless about what tasks are performed by which regions of the brain. The easiest way for them to get a handle on this mystery was to stimulate or even remove different parts of animal brains to see what would happen . . . or not happen. For example, if you remove a piece of a rat brain and the rat can't see anymore, you know that the piece you removed has something to do with vision.

But those early brain tinkerers noticed that removing or stimulating many sections of the brain didn't have any clear effect, which meant that they couldn't say what, if anything, those parts do. So, while it was true at the time to say that a large percentage of the brain didn't have a *known* function, it was a huge leap in logic to say that this chunk didn't do anything at all. Somebody took that leap, evidently, and the idea stuck.

Many have blamed the American psychologist William James for popularizing the notion. In a 1907 essay, "The Energies of Men," James said, "We are making use of only a small part of our possible mental and physical resources," and he observed that people frequently fail to reach their full potential. But James's point was that the habitual patterns of our thought limit us, not that there are actual physical pieces of our brains that are idle.

In any case, it's clear why the myth is so persistent. Whether you envision developing ESP or memorizing all 180 *Seinfeld* episodes, it's exciting to daydream about having ten times the brainpower. Psychics, advertisers, news anchors, and inspirational speakers love the idea so much that they just can't let it go.

But your brain does have untapped potential, in the sense that you'll never think all the thoughts you could possibly think (there are virtually unlimited patterns of neural connection). And the brain might have greater potential than we previously thought, thanks to a phenomenon called neuroplasticity—the brain's ability to restructure itself to develop new, remarkable abilities. For example, patients who have suffered damage to the vestibular system in their inner ears have been able to reestablish balance by interpreting visual signals from a strip of electrodes on their tongue. The science of neuroplasticity is still young, and while it isn't likely to lead to widespread mental spoon-bending skills, it could certainly expand our notions of the brain's capabilities. You might just turn into a super-genius after all.

IS BREAKFAST REALLY THE MOST IMPORTANT MEAL OF THE DAY?

If your idea of breakfast is a double martini, probably not. Otherwise, the answer is yes. Evidence suggests that kicking the day off with a reasonably healthy meal is one of the best things you can do for your body.

The clearest benefit to breakfast is that it helps to keep your metabolism humming along at the right rate. Why? If you go too long without eating, you risk triggering a starvation reflex in your body. We evolved to live in the wild, which means that our bodies don't know anything about dieting or rushing off to work or any of the other modern-day reasons for skipping meals. On a cellular level, not eating for a long period of time indicates to your body that there's no food around. As a precaution against potential starvation, your energy level drops and you start saving up energy in the form of fat.

Breakfast, then, is vital because when you wake up, you've already gone a long time without eating. Let's say that you have an evening snack at nine o'clock and then don't eat until lunchtime the next day. That's fifteen hours without food—plenty of time for glucose levels to fall and for your body to start preparing for a perceived dearth of food in the future. The upshot? You're more sluggish, and the calories that you consume at lunch probably produce more fat than they would otherwise. Even a healthy lunch might not get your glucose levels back to where they should be, so you may remain sluggish for the rest of the afternoon.

The consequences of skipping breakfast don't end there. In a Harvard Medical School study that was published in 2003, researchers found that people who skip breakfast are three times more likely to be obese than those who eat a meal first thing in the morning. Furthermore, they're twice as likely to develop problems with blood sugar, which can increase the risks of diabetes and heart disease. Of course, not all breakfasts are created equal. Research suggests that the best bet is to eat relatively small portions that contain low-fat complex carbohydrates (like whole grain cereal) and a little protein (yogurt or milk).

ARE FARMER'S ALMANACS MORE ACCURATE THAN THE LOCAL WEATHERMAN?

Well, they are more accurate when it comes to reporting blue-ribbon casserole recipes or amazing fishing stories. As for predicting the weather? Not so much. The two leading farmer's almanacs are *Farmers' Almanac*, sold every year since 1818, and *The Old Farmer's Almanac*, sold every year since 1792. Both publish long-range weather predictions that they create using secret formulas, supposedly based in part on sunspot activity. And both claim to be 80 percent accurate or better. The problem is that the predictions are vague enough that assessing their accuracy is difficult.

For example, *The Old Farmer's Almanac*'s regional forecasts provide average temperatures and precipitation amounts for each month, with simple, impressionistic descriptions (e.g., "sunny, comfortable") for three- to seven-day blocks. So if it rains on one day in a seven-day block, should a "sunny" prediction be considered accurate?

It's not as hard as you might think for the almanac writers to hit the mark—they can do well just by looking at historical averages. For example, they can say with some authority that December in Minnesota will be cold and icy, and they can probably even guess an average temperature within five or ten degrees. Historical trends, then, are certainly a big part of their secret formulas. Independent analyses suggest that the specific predictions in the almanacs are accurate a little more than half of the time, at best. For example, in 2004, meteorologist Nick Bond compared thirteen years of verifiable predictions from *The Old Farmer's Almanac* to the meteorological record. He concluded that the almanac was accurate about 50 percent of the time, which put it on par with random guessing.

How does that stack up against the forecast on your local news? Believe it or not, your weatherman's seven-day forecast might not be much more accurate than the almanac's. But one- to three-day forecasts are significantly more reliable, according to ForecastAdvisor.com, a Web site that tracks predictions from the major forecasting services. A sampling of its accuracy rankings shows that yearly scores typically fall between 70 and 85 percent, depending on the city. And these are fairly strict assessments of specific, daily predictions for precipitation and high and low temperatures, information that is more detailed than what the almanacs provide.

Then again, you can't take the local weatherman with you to the can. Every copy of *The Old Farmer's Almanac* has a hole in the upper left corner so that you can hang it on an outhouse nail.

HOW LONG WOULD IT TAKE A SCHOOL OF PIRANHAS TO FINISH OFF A COW?

How big is the cow? How many piranhas—and how hungry are they? Like sharks, piranhas are drawn to blood; they're killers from the moment they are born. And it's true—a pack of piranhas can indeed strip the flesh from a much larger animal, such as a cow. The estimated time it would take to skeletonize a cow varies. Some sources claim it would take less than a minute; others say up to five minutes. But marine biologists call these estimates exaggerations. The piranha has a fearsome, tooth-filled grin—but under normal circumstances, it is not considered overly aggressive.

In the United States, the legend of the ravenous piranha began with Theodore Roosevelt's 1913 trip to South America. He returned full of stories, many of which concerned the carnivorous fish. It is thought that the Brazilian tour guides who were charged with showing President Roosevelt a good time had a joke at his expense by making piranhas out to be more dangerous than they are. There was an incident in which a cow was lowered into a branch of the Rio Aripuana that was teeming with piranhas, and the outcome was every bit as grisly as legend says. But some vital facts were left out of the story. For one, the cow was sick and bleeding, which spurred the fish into a frenzy. Furthermore, the piranhas were isolated, hungry, and ornery. They saw a meal and went nuts—and we've been talking about it ever since.

Modern jungle-dwellers don't typically see piranhas as a danger. The fish usually feed on small animals—other fish, frogs, and baby caimans. It's not uncommon for a human to be bitten by a piranha, but these wounds are usually small and singular. Little flesh lost, little harm done—the sated fish and the startled human go their separate ways.

Of course, this isn't to say that piranhas lack the capacity to wreak havoc. Piranhas are known to be most vicious during the dry season. They are believed to travel in large schools for the purpose of protection, and they stimulate one another at feeding time. In light of this information, there are instances when you don't want to get anywhere near a piranha. If you have an open wound, for instance, it might be a good idea to forego that afternoon dip in the Rio Aripuana.

WHY ISN'T THE WHOLE PLANE MADE OF THE SAME STUFF AS THE BLACK BOX?

Planes, believe it or not, are pretty lightweight. They're built with light metals, such as aluminum. The newer ones are built with even lighter composite materials and plastics. This allows them to be fairly sturdy without adding too much weight.

If planes were made of the same stuff as the black box, they just wouldn't get off the ground. But let's backtrack a bit here. The term "black box" is a little misleading. What the media refer to as a "black box" is actually two boxes: the Flight Data Recorder (FDR), which records altitude, speed, magnetic heading, and so on; and the Cockpit Voice Recorder (CVR), which records the sounds in the cockpit (presumably ensuring that pilots are on their best behavior all the time). What's more, these boxes are generally bright orange, making them easier to find after a crash. "Black" box either comes from older models that were black or from the charred and/or damaged states of the boxes after a crash.

Whatever the reason behind the name, black boxes are sturdy little things. They carry a bunch of microchips and memory banks encased in protective stainless steel. The protective casing is about a quarter-inch thick, which makes the boxes really heavy. Furthermore, black boxes are not necessarily indestructible—they usually remain intact after a crash partially because they are well placed. They're generally put in the tail of the plane, which often doesn't bear the brunt of a crash.

Even with this extra protection, black boxes sometimes don't survive a plane crash. Still, they typically have been useful, though not so useful that you'd want to build an entire plane with their stainless steel casings.

IS IT TRUE THAT BED BUGS BITE?

You better believe they do. In fact, it's pretty much the only thing they do.

A brownish-red, flat, and oval-shaped wingless insect, the common bed bug (*Cimex lectularius* if you're a Latin lover) grows to about a quarter-inch in length and feeds exclusively on the blood of animals. This includes you, sleepyhead. Bed bugs are nocturnal, hiding in cracks and crevices during the day and emerging at night to feed on any nearby, tasty host. They use an elongated beak, or *proboscis*, to puncture the skin and can spend three to ten minutes drawing blood. Often, the victim never feels a thing.

If you awake with itchy, reddish welts on your skin, it's possible that you were the main course at a bed-bug feast. But symptoms vary, and some people don't react to the bites at all. Thankfully, under normal circumstances, bites from bed bugs don't spread disease, just a measure of discomfort.

Bed bugs don't prey exclusively on humans—they can also be found around the nests of birds and bats, for example. But they have demonstrated an enduring affinity for people: Literary references to bed bugs date to the days of Aristotle. The little suckers were on the run in America in the years following World War II, however. The rise of such household cleaning staples as vacuum cleaners and pesticides helped diminish their forces.

But as pesticides with the broad-spectrum killer DDT were replaced by more specialized products tailored specifically for such pests as roaches and ants, bed bugs regained their foothold. And because they travel well in clothing and luggage, they've been slowly reintroduced into North America, most notably in hotels (and not just the cheap ones), homes, offices, and hospitals. "Don't let the bed bugs bite" isn't just a quaint saying. These pesky predators are back in business.

ARE NICKELS MADE OF NICKEL?

What do you think they're made of, wood?

The original U.S. five-cent piece was made of silver, at a time when all coins were required by law to be made of gold, silver, or copper. That silver five-cent piece was called a "half disme." ("Disme" was pronounced "dime." This was at a time, apparently, when some coins were required by law to have odd, confusingly spelled names.)

Congress—in its perennial effort to cause confusion, create waste, and operate with an overall lack of efficiency— ordered the U.S. Mint to begin producing a new five-cent piece in 1866, although production of the now fully dissed half disme continued for another seven years. Made from nickel and copper, this new five-cent coin was significantly larger than the half disme, because nickel was relatively cheap compared to silver. Congress immediately dubbed the new coin the "nisckel." (Okay, we made up that last part.) To this day, the American nickel coin is made of nickel—25 percent nickel, to be exact—and copper.

But let's return to wood for a moment. The reference to wooden nickels at the top of this entry might not be as preposterous as it seems. According to the Wooden Nickel Historical Museum, round wooden coins were issued in the early 1930s by the chamber of commerce of Blaine, Washington, following the failure of a local bank. These wooden coins, which included nickels, are considered the first legal wooden money and are now valuable collector's items.

Of course, there's the well-known phrase, "Don't take any wooden nickels." This saying is believed to have originated in the early twentieth century when commemorative wooden tokens, about the shape and size of nickels, were sometimes issued as currency to be used at exhibitions or fairs. Once the event closed, the "coins" became worthless, leaving owners of any unused wooden nickels feeling as if they'd been scammed.

HOW DO DICTIONARY WRITERS KNOW HOW TO SPELL A WORD?

How would you know if they didn't?

Dictionary writers are generally a bunch of respected scholars and smart people who are each hired to work on small sections of the dictionary (say, all the words from "ban-" to "bec-"). Not surprisingly, editing a dictionary generally requires a large amount of time devoted to reading—anything and everything. Dictionary editors might scan whatever they read for new words that are becoming popular, new uses of old words, and any spelling variants. Once that's done, the entries might be recorded in a massive database, and perhaps kept in hard copy. This database can provide an easy reference for research about words.

A word is usually not added to the dictionary until a determination has been made that it is widely used by various sources. The choice of spelling is based on all the examples, with the most common spelling being the one used. The dictionary may also have general "house rules" about how to spell words.

Dictionary editors have some discretion in choosing spellings. An example of this is the American spelling of "color" compared to the British spelling, "colour," which goes back to Noah Webster, editor of the first American dictionary.

One of Webster's pet peeves was when a word appeared to have a misleading or overly complicated spelling—too many silent letters, for example. He believed that American spelling should reflect the forthright values of the new republic, emphasizing logical consistency and spartan simplicity. In this instance, he tried to simplify the spelling by dropping the "u" from this word and others like it ("humour," for example, became "humor"). The American public concurred, and the new spelling stuck. This wasn't the case, however, with some of his other reforms, such as "tung" for "tongue" and "wimmen" for "women."

Now that the printed word is ubiquitous, there are fewer spelling variations than in the distant past, when scribes would typically try to spell words according to how they heard them spoken, with no dictionaries—and certainly no online search engines—for checking the really tough ones. Still, today's dictionary writers have their work cut out for them. By some estimates, the English language has between 750,000 and 1,250,000 words.

HOW DO DOGS REMEMBER WHERE THEY BURY THEIR BONES?

Ever watched your dog bury a bone? After covering its treasure with dirt, it'll press its nose into the ground as if it's literally tamping the soil down with its snout. You can always tell when a dog's been digging: that dirty nose is a dead giveaway.

So how does a dog find its buried treasure weeks or maybe months later? It follows its nose. The enzymes that are released by decomposing bones, especially raw ones, give off a distinctive odor. We can't smell it, but a dog certainly can—dogs can smell one thousand to ten thousand times better than humans can.

A dog that's looking for its buried bone will sniff around, keeping its nose close to the ground until it finds the exact spot. Incidentally, this ability to detect decomposing bones is what enables dogs to help law enforcement officials find corpses. According to California's Institute for Canine

Forensics, dogs are even used at archaeological digs to help locate ancient burial grounds.

A dog's propensity for burying bones is what zoologists call cache behavior. It's also found among wolves, wild dogs, and foxes. When a kill is too large to be devoured at a single sitting, these animals bury what they can't eat in safe places. Canines are highly territorial. Your dog will never bury its bones in another dog's yard, though it may try to sneak in and dig up its neighbor's cache on the sly. Wild canines also bury food in areas that they have marked as their own, which they defend fiercely. During lean times, they will dig up their hidden food stores—it's sort of like having something set aside for the proverbial rainy day.

Do dogs always retrieve the bones they bury? Not necessarily. Cache behavior is an important survival technique for canines in the wild, but well-fed domestic pets may simply have no need for their buried leftovers. Furthermore, cooked bones don't hold the same allure as raw ones—they disintegrate faster, and their scent is sometimes masked by the odors of the surrounding soil.

If your yard is full of unsightly holes, you're probably wondering how you can stop your dog from burying bones everywhere. Well, the cache instinct is so powerful that there isn't too much you can do to prevent it. As any experienced dog owner can tell you, a dog will always bury something. If Fido doesn't have a bone, a favorite toy or even your favorite running shoe will do the trick. Indoor dogs will often hide their toys under beds, behind curtains, or behind sofa cushions. Some veterinarians recommend giving a dog its own sandbox or a pile of pillows where it can "play" at hiding and seeking.

These vets add that encouraging cache behavior can be a great interactive way of getting to know your pet better.

So join the fun. Instead of punishing your dog for doing what comes naturally, roll up your sleeves, grab that tattered old stinky sneaker, and dig in.

WHAT CAUSES THE WIND TO BLOW?

Judging by some of the graphics your local TV weather person uses during the nightly forecast, you'd think that wind is caused by cartoon clouds that expand their billowy cheeks and blow. But don't believe it.

Wind is the result of Earth's atmosphere constantly trying (and failing) to maintain equilibrium. The sun warms the atmosphere and Earth's surface, but that warmth is spread unevenly. This inconsistent heating creates global patterns of high and low air pressure. Wherever there are differences in atmospheric pressure, air rushes from the high-pressure areas to the low-pressure regions to try to make up the difference. This mass movement of air creates wind.

The patterns of these vast air movements vary based on a number of factors. Close to the planet's surface, winds rotate around low-pressure areas (called cyclones) and high-pressure areas (anticyclones). Meanwhile, up in the atmosphere, ridges of high pressure and troughs of low pressure create waves that push air around and often dictate the travel of the cyclones that are close to the ground. In addition, certain geographic features such as mountains or bodies of water create local wind systems. Even the rotation of the planet has an effect on the way that the air flows.

It all makes weather prediction kind of a crapshoot— especially for people who make drawings of wind-blowing clouds for a living. And don't even get us started on the ludicrous notion that the sun would ever actually need to wear sunglasses.

ARE OWLS REALLY WISE?

The owl is fairly unique among birds. Its eyes are on the front of its head instead of on the sides like most birds. If an owl wants to look sideways, it can turn its head about three quarters of the way around. However, the trait with which we most commonly associate owls is wisdom. Are owls really all that wise?

Well, it depends on your point of reference. If you're comparing them to other birds, owls do have impressive vision and hunting skills. They fly so quietly that snapped-up mice generally don't know what hit them. But if you talk to wildlife rehabilitators and others who work with owls on a regular basis, "wisdom" and "intelligence" aren't two words you're likely to hear. Other birds, such as crows, are much easier to train.

The owl's reputation comes from its association with Athena, the Greek goddess of wisdom. In one myth, Athena chose the owl as her favorite bird because of its somber appearance and demeanor. Athena was also a warrior, and the owl was viewed as a symbol of protection in battle; if an owl was sighted from the battlefield, it was considered an omen of victory. Because of the link to Athena, owls were considered sacred in ancient Greece. Many Greek coins bear images of owls, and the owl is used to represent Athena herself, in addition to showing up next to her in art and sculpture. Some scholars believe that Athena may have originally been a bird or a bird-like goddess. In legend and mythology, then, the owl is indeed wise. But in reality, not so much.

CAN YOU GO BLIND LOOKING AT A SOLAR ECLIPSE?

This one seems to have B.S. written all over it. In elementary school, you were probably terrorized by teachers and other dour adults who warned against looking directly at a solar eclipse. But if this danger were real, wouldn't there be blind people everywhere? Consider: it's the day of the solar eclipse, the sky starts to get really dark, you automatically look up to see what's going on, and boom—you're poking your way around with a white cane for the rest of your life. Where's the logic? Well, amazingly, the concept here isn't a complete load.

First off, staring at the sun at any time isn't a good idea. Prolonged exposure to the ultraviolet radiation from the sun can damage the nerve endings in the eye, leading to vision problems such as spotting, blurriness, and, in extreme cases, blindness. Exposing the retina to intense visible light causes damage to its light-sensitive rod and cone cells. The light can trigger a series of complex chemical reactions within the cells that damages their ability to respond to a visual stimulus and, in extreme cases, can destroy them. There are many factors that affect how your eyes will respond to this kind of abuse, including the size and color of your eyes, preexisting eye problems, and the angle of the sun.

As a result, it is difficult to say exactly how long one can look at the sun without injury, but you should try to limit your exposure to less than a minute. While this might not seem like much time, think about how difficult and painful it is to keep your eyes trained on the sun for even ten seconds. What makes solar eclipses so dangerous is that the stare-prohibiting glare of the sun is greatly diminished.

Just how dangerous are eclipses? Staring at one won't cause instant blindness. Furthermore, the term "blindness" is a bit of an overstatement—eye impairments can be as minor as a slight discoloration in the visual field. This type of damage typically is temporary, and many people recover their normal vision within a few weeks.

So the warnings from your grade-school teachers were slightly exaggerated. Still, their general message was sound: It's never a bright idea to stare at that bright ball in the sky.

WHY ARE BULLS ENRAGED BY THE COLOR RED?

Red has been the color of choice of bullfighters for centuries. Their bright capes are used to incite their bovine opponents into spectacular rages. In fact, the phrase "seeing red" is believed to have originated from the fury that the color seems to provoke in the bull. What is it about red that ticks off bulls?

The amazing truth is: nothing. Bulls are partially color-blind and don't respond to the color red at all. The red color of the cape is just eye candy for the audience, much like the bullfighter's *traje de luces* (suit of lights).

Then is it the motion of the cape that infuriates the bull? Again, the truth is: not really. There's not a lot that the matador needs to do to make the bull angry—it's in pretty bad humor before it even enters the ring. These bulls aren't bred to take quiet walks in the park on Sunday afternoons. No, they are selected because they exhibit violent and aggressive behavior. By the time they hit the bullfighting arena, just about anything will set them off.

We're talking about bulls that have personalities like John McEnroe. The color red doesn't make them angry— *everything* makes them angry. Then again, the bullfighter plunging his sword into the bull's neck might have something to do with the beast's nasty disposition, too.

HOW DO YOU PASS AN ACID TEST?

Remember the first time you met your girlfriend's father? The interrogation? The stammering? The urge to run away? That was an acid test. No actual acid was involved, of course. But the experience could hardly have been worse had he applied burning chemicals to your skin.

An acid test is administered to gauge authenticity. The term is borrowed from metallurgy, specifically gold mining. A quick way to distinguish real gold from fool's gold is to subject it to an acid test: Real gold doused with acid won't dissolve.

When we pass an acid test, we have demonstrated that we are genuine, that our intentions are pure. Indeed, if you got your girlfriend home on time after that first parental encounter, you were probably golden—at least until the next date.

Now, if your girlfriend's father happened to be Timothy Leary, your acid test might have included vivid colors, incoherent conversation, and uncontrolled laughter. But chances are you wouldn't have remembered much of it.

CAN CATS SUFFOCATE BABIES BY TAKING AWAY THEIR BREATH?

No, but that doesn't make the myth any less interesting. Its origin may lie with the legend of the succubus, a demonic nocturnal spirit, usually feminine, that sucks life from its victims. With their eerie eyes, night-stalking habits, and association with witches, cats fit the succubus profile.

Before much was known about sudden infant death syndrome (SIDS), a person who discovered a cat close to a dead baby might have been quick to assume that the feline had something to do with it. In fact, in 1791, a coroner in Plymouth, England, ruled that a cat killed a child by sucking the child's breath. The report does not mention evidence that may have been gathered to support this conclusion—or exactly how a cat could be capable of such a feat.

On December 21, 2000, Nicola Payne of London found her six-week-old son dead in his crib with the family cat curled up next to him. The media reported that the cat had suffocated the baby by lying on his face. But an investigation did not reveal cat hair in the infant's nose, mouth, or airways: Pathologists concluded that SIDS was the cause.

Indeed, there are *no* verifiable cases of cats causing infant deaths. However, cats are attracted to warm, cozy places like cribs, so veterinarians and pediatricians recommend that newborn babies and cats be kept apart when an adult is not present. A cat may be aroused by the scent of milk on a baby's breath and attempt to explore the source of the odor. Or it may mistake a baby's crying for the mewing of a rival feline and become aggressive. With a little common sense and patience, cats and tots can get along just fine, as millions of happy feline-owning parents can verify.

WHAT'S THE DIFFERENCE BETWEEN A PLANT AND A WEED?

One man's weed is another man's salad. Indeed, the simplest definition of a weed is a plant you don't like that's in the midst of plants you do like. Take good old ground ivy. In your yard's natural area, it's a lovely ground cover; in your garden, it's a strangling weed. Dandelions, meanwhile, can be used for medicinal purposes, and they're also edible. Add a little bacon, sliced hardboiled egg, chopped onion, and a dash of vinegar, and, mmm, you have a salad. On American lawns, however, dandelions are almost universally considered a hated weed.

A weed is a nuisance in a lawn or garden simply because it competes for sun, water, and nutrients with the plants that you have decided should grow there. Weeds are hardy and maddeningly adaptable. They can be annuals, like crabgrass, which produces seeds for one season; they'll drive you nuts and then die off.

Then there are the biennials, which bloom and then go dormant for two years. The classy sounding Queen Anne's lace, also known as the wild carrot, is a biennial weed.

Perennial weeds are the guests that won't leave. They hunker down and mooch off the "good" plants. They're often buggers to get rid of. Dandelions are classic perennials and have a highly effective seed-spreading system—every time a breeze or a kid blows the white puffy seeds off a dandelion, hundreds of opportunities for new dandelion plants fly through the air.

If you've decided that the thing growing in your yard is a weed and not a plant, how do you kill it? You can douse it with herbicides (be careful not to hurt the "good plants") or smother it with newspaper, plastic, or landscaping cloth. Or you can yank it from the ground, but remember that many weeds are very resilient, and if a morsel of root is left behind, it'll return again and again, like *Rocky* movies. The alternative is to simply relax, fry up some bacon, dice an onion, and get out the salad bowls.

DID THAT REALLY NEED TO BE INVENTED?

"

The guy who invented the first wheel was an idiot. The guy who invented the other three, he was a genius.

—Sid Caesar

"

Invented things didn't exist before they were invented. They may meet a pressing, timeless human need—such as, you know, the electric foot-callus sander—but they weren't around until a light bulb winked on in someone's head. Or, in some cases, accidentally exploded. An invention may grow in scope (heh) to launch the mouthwash industry. It may open the lid (heh) on corollary inventions like can openers. Or it might suddenly go off (heh) and become a permanent part of daily life despite the fact that no one really likes alarm clocks. (Okay, we'll stop.) And along with the nifty ideas and inspired accidents are those other inventions—the head-scratchers that make us wonder about the warped souls capable of thinking them up in the first place.

WHO CAN WE BLAME
FOR THE MULLET?

The mullet was rearing its ugly head as long ago as the Trojan War, around 1200 BC. Indeed, the first documented account of the short-hair-around-the-face, long-hair-covering-the-neck-in-back look is in *The Iliad*. Homer relates that the fierce, spear-carrying Abantes warriors wore their tresses long and flowing, but with "their forelocks cropped."

While mullet-like hairstyles have appeared since then (think of Gainsborough's eighteenth-century "Blue Boy" painting), rock stars made it popular in the early 1970s. David Bowie's 1972 Ziggy Stardust character cut his short in front and long in back, and dyed it bright orange to complete the look. Beatles legend Paul McCartney sported a tame mullet when he launched his new band, Wings, in 1971. The style caught on—though it wasn't yet called the mullet.

Men and women, from punky Lou Reed to prissy Florence Henderson, sported variations in the 1970s. In the 1980s, movie stars Brad Pitt and Mel Gibson and TV's Richard Dean Anderson (*MacGyver*) proudly wore mullets. Singers Billy Ray Cyrus and Michael Bolton and tennis ace Andre Agassi were among celebrities who ushered the mullet into the 1990s. By the time David Spade wore one in the 2001 movie *Joe Dirt*, the look had become linked with lounge lizards and seedy ne'er-do-wells. Today, it's affectionately celebrated on several Web sites.

The mullet, which is essentially two haircuts in one, has many names. It's sometimes called the 10/90: 10 percent of the hair in front, 90 percent in back. It's also known as the ape drape, hockey hair, and the Tennessee top hat. "Business up front, party in the back" is both a nickname and a description.

No one is sure who started calling the hairdo a mullet. "Mullethead" was an insult in Mark Twain's day—it's what he called dimwits in *The Adventures of Huckleberry Finn*—but the term referred to mullet fish. Today, it refers to hair . . . but it's still kind of an insult.

IF YOU THOUGHT IT WAS INVENTED AT THE SAME TIME AS THE TIN CAN . . .

You'd be wrong. The can opener was certainly a sharp invention, but it was also long overdue.

Before the can opener, there was a revolutionary (albeit somewhat half-baked) invention called the can. The process for canning foodstuffs was patented by Peter Durand of Britain in 1810, and the first commercial canning factory opened three years later. The British Army quickly became a leading customer for the innovative product. After all, the can greatly simplified the logistics of keeping the nation's soldiers fed. In 1846, a new machine that could produce 60 cans per hour increased the rate of production for tinned food tenfold. Life made easier through the wonders of technology, right?

Well, not exactly. In all that time, no one came up with a way to address the most serious drawback of this perfectly sealed, air-tight, solid-iron container: It was incredibly difficult to open! In fact, some cans actually came with instructions that read, "Cut 'round the top near the outer edge with a chisel and hammer."

It wasn't until the middle of the century—when manufacturers devised methods for producing thinner cans made of steel—that there was any hope of creating a simple and safe way to open them. In 1858, Ezra Warner of Connecticut patented the first functional can opener, a bulky thing resembling a bent bayonet that you shoved through the top of the can and then carefully forced around the lid. It was an improvement, no doubt, but still a tiresome and potentially dangerous way to get at your potted meat.

Then, in 1870, a full 60 years after the canning process was perfected, William Lyman designed an easy-to-use wheeled blade that could cut a can open as it rolled around the edge of the lid—essentially the same function as that of the can openers we use today. The next two big inventions in can-opening technology were a long time coming: The electric can opener appeared in the 1930s, and pull-open cans arrived in 1966.

WHY WOULD ANYONE
BUY THAT?

For the same reason anyone bought cars with fins or transistor radios: The aluminum Christmas tree was once the latest high-tech, shiny, groovy gadget.

On a cold and gray Chicago morning in December 1958, Tom Gannon saw a unique, homemade metal tree in a Christmas display at a Ben Franklin five-and-dime discount store. The favorably impressed Gannon was the toy sales manager of the Aluminum Specialty Company of Manitowoc, Wisconsin—and by the following Christmas, his firm had the aluminum Christmas tree on the market. It was a hit. Over the next ten years, Aluminum Specialty Company sold more than one million Evergleam trees in sizes ranging from two to eight feet tall. At least forty other companies jumped on the bandwagon, and aluminum trees were manufactured through the 1970s.

The trees were modern and flashy. Their metallic sheen complemented any color scheme, and ornaments glittered off the sparkling boughs. They also were reusable—individual branches fit into holes in the trunk, so that when the holidays were over, the whole bundle of holiday cheer could be carefully taken apart and shoved in the attic until next Christmas. There was just one downside: The electrical conductivity of the branches made strands of Christmas lights a no-no. But some owners used rotating floodlights to bathe their trees in different tints as a substitute for that tradition.

So who killed the aluminum Christmas tree? One unlikely suspect is a certain prematurely bald youngster from the funny pages. In 1965, CBS premiered *A Charlie Brown Christmas*. The animated film used a big pink aluminum tree as a symbol of yuletide commercialism and fakery. Was it coincidence that the popularity of aluminum trees took a nosedive soon after? Whatever the cause, suddenly you couldn't give aluminum trees away. Tastes changed, and everyone wanted a natural, sweet-smelling, green Christmas tree. Even fake trees went green.

Today the vintage aluminum models are sought-after collectibles, and nostalgic reproductions of aluminum trees go in and out of fashion. Like fins on cars, aluminum trees evoke a specific era. Those who remember such trees from their childhoods look at them fondly—for about five minutes. Then they wonder, "What was I thinking?"

AN ALARMING INNOVATION

Historians say the Greeks devised an alarm clock as early as 250 BC. It used rising water to trigger a mechanical whistle. The Germans devised a large iron wall piece rigged with bronze bells in the 15th century. And chimes have sounded on clocks since the Middle Ages; the word "clock" even comes from the French word *cloche*, meaning "far too early to rise." Just kidding. It means "bell."

But the modern alarm clock we all know and hate got its start in Concord, New Hampshire, in 1787, courtesy of 26-year-old clockmaker and staunch early riser, Levi Hutchins. Yet without the sun to wake him in the wee hours, Hutchins tended to oversleep. So he gutted a large brass clock, placed the innards inside a pine cabinet, and inserted a gear tripped to sound at 4 a.m. (However, it couldn't be set for any other time.)

Hutchins's idea worked, but he never patented it. That credit goes to the Seth Thomas Company, which in 1876 patented a bedside windup alarm clock that could be set for any hour. Eighty years later, General Electric-Telechron introduced the snooze alarm (thank goodness).

DR. GUILLOTIN GETS AHEAD

In the midst of the myth and mayhem of the French Revolution, we find the guillotine, a singularly efficient invention if you need to lop off a lot of heads quickly. Before we look at the device, however, let's clear up a misconception: Dr. Joseph-Ignace Guillotin did not invent the guillotine. Mechanical beheading devices had long been used in Germany, Italy, Scotland, and elsewhere, though it was the French who made them (in)famous.

The respected physician, a member of the French National Assembly, opposed the death penalty. However, he realized that public executions weren't going away, so he sought a more "humane" alternative to being drawn and quartered, which was the usual way that impoverished criminals were put to death. A quick beheading, Guillotin argued, was far more merciful than being hacked apart. And it had the added benefit of making executions socially equal, since beheading had been, until that time, the method of execution only for aristocratic convicts who could buy themselves a quicker death.

So Guillotin approached a German engineer named Tobias Schmidt, who built a prototype of the guillotine. For a smoother cut, Schmidt suggested a diagonal blade rather than the traditional round blade. Not much later, the new civilian assembly rewrote the penal code to make beheading by guillotine the official method of execution for all convicted criminals—and there were a lot of them. The first person to lose his head was Nicolas Jacques Pelletie, who was guillotined at Place de Greve on April 25, 1792. King Louis XVI felt the blade a year later, and thousands more followed.

INVENTING THE NEED
FOR LISTERINE

Some 40 years after Listerine's invention, marketing gurus finally figured out how to sell it to Jane and Joe Average: Tell Jane that if she didn't cure her toxic breath, Joe wouldn't kiss her.

NOT BY LISTER?

Surgery was a filthy business in the 19th century. U.S. President James Garfield died from the crude probings of his doctors' bare, germy fingers as they scrounged around his abdomen trying to fish out an assassin's bullet—and Garfield had the finest medical care of the day. The worst was a Dante's *Inferno* of squalor, amputation, infection, and gangrene. In wartime, a bullet to the gut generally meant an agonizing death that surgery would merely hasten.

Into that breach stepped Dr. Joseph Lister, an English doctor who advised doctors to wear gloves, wash their hands, and sanitize their instruments. It was that simple. The mortality rate dropped so far that a grateful Queen Victoria made Lister a baron. But later generations would most frequently associate him with a mouthwash he didn't invent and probably never used.

THEN WHO DID?

Dr. Joseph Lawrence and Jordan Lambert first whipped up a batch of surgical disinfectant in 1879—a blend of thymol, menthol, eucalyptol, and methyl salicylate in grain alcohol.

It needed a name. Did the inventors name it after Lister to honor him or to ride on his famous coattails? That depends on your opinion of the inventors' motives, but the profit motive surely drove Listerine's invention and marketing. There's no evidence that Dr. Lister ever received a penny for the appropriation of his name, nor that he complained or cared. A devout man of science and medicine, Lister didn't seek riches.

HERE COMES THE MARKETING

In 1884, Lambert formed the Lambert Company to sell Listerine. By 1895, it was clear that Listerine did a quick, safe job of wiping out oral bacteria, so Lambert started hawking it to dentists as well. One might say that Western medicine washed away centuries of sin with a baptism in Listerine.

IF DUELS WERE STILL LEGAL, YOUR BREATH WOULD BE LETHAL

By 1914, Lambert's son Gerard was calling the shots for Listerine. In an era of snake-oil concoctions with names like Spurrier's Powders, Kvak's Pills, and Boga's Tonic, which promised to cure anything from baldness and "female complaints" to rheumatism and colds yet conferred no actual health benefit, Listerine was the exception—*it actually did something useful.*

Gerard started selling Listerine over the counter as a mouthwash, thus inventing the category . . . and soon realized he had to invent the problem. His new advertising focused on halitosis, or bad breath, and played on the idea (often well-founded, granted) that oblivious persons with poor dental habits might be offending everyone with their dragon breath.

The cure? You know what it was. Americans started rinsing their mouths with medical disinfectant. The Lambert Company's annual revenues went from $115,000 to $8 million in seven years. Wish we could bust a marketing move like Gerard Lambert. Today, Listerine comes in a variety of flavors, but you can still buy the old-school version. It hasn't changed much, if at all, since Jordan Lambert started selling it as a surgical sanitizer.

OF WHALEBONES AND WOMEN

The first ancestress of the corset, worn from the mid-15th through the late 16th centuries, was a heavy under-bodice that laced up the sides or the front. A tapered "busk" of horn or whalebone was inserted in the front of the bodice to keep it rigid. At some point, whalebone was added to the sides and back. Interestingly, scholars report that the corset-wearers of the period were not necessarily uncomfortable— the infamously painful period of corsetry occurred later during the 19th century.

Boned bodices became fully boned stays in the late 17th century, when the preferred silhouette was long and narrow rather than broad and stiff. Stays that produced a slender line required more seams, tapering down to the waistline. By the middle of the 18th century, extra shaping bones were sewn into stays to give the breasts some *oomph* and keep the back flat. Whalebone strips were laid diagonally on the sides to make the body long and narrow. Pregnant women were given a break—their stays laced at the sides, allowing more room.

CHANGING STYLES

Women could breathe a little easier at the end of the 18th century. The accessibility of fine cottons from India allowed for a looser style using the natural drape of the fabric. Sashes narrowed and waistlines rose. At first, women wore lighter stays under the new styles, made with more pliable materials and fewer bones. By the beginning of the 19th century, however, draped Greek statues were the ideal. Light muslin dresses clung to the body and underclothes that could spoil the silhouette were abandoned—at least in theory. In practice, even slender women often wore a cotton lining with two side pieces that fastened under the breasts, providing some support; heavier women experimented with stays that came down over the hips and tightly-fitted knitted silk body garments.

The respite was brief. A new silhouette emphasizing full skirts and narrow waists came into fashion with the end of the Napoleonic War, bringing the first true corset with it and ushering in the tight-lacing fad. Victorian women wanted tiny, wasplike waists, and the new corsets could give them that desirable figure. Usually laced up the back, the corset had a broad busk in the center front and narrow strips of whalebone at the back and sides. Gussets on the front at the top of the corset and on each side at the base produced roundness at the bust and the hips, emphasizing the smallness of the waist.

Over time, corsets became heavier and even more restricting. Rubber-coated steel replaced the lighter, more pliable whalebone. Further changes in silhouette, including the bustle in the 1870s and the "S-curve" of the early 1900s, all exaggerated and distorted the female shape, requiring more heavily boned corsets.

Women's underwear underwent a much-needed simplification in the 20th century. Steel shortages during World War I and the introduction of rubberized elastic allowed women some freedom from tight stays. Finally, the free-for-all loose fashions of the 1920s marked the demise of the corset.

ALL SHOOK UP

Got an achy back? Suffering from sleepless nights? Simply bored in your motel room? Put Magic Fingers to work!

In the 1960s, although motel rooms were cheap, independent motel owners still had to be mindful of their competition. After the Motel 6 chain started adding free color televisions, telephones, and coffee makers to its rooms, competitors were left scrambling for amenities to add value to their rooms. Enter the magic machine.

GENTLY SHAKE YOU TO SLEEP

John Houghtaling invented Magic Fingers in 1958; initially it was sold as a therapeutic device guaranteed to solve many of the medical problems that occur with modern travel: back pain, stress, and sleeplessness. In reality, it was nothing more than a little electric motor that, when fastened to the underside of a mattress, shook the guest until they either fell asleep or were pitched off the bed. Originally selling for more than $200, the Magic Fingers included not only the vibrator but the mattress as well.

After months of dismal sales, Houghtaling realized that replacing the mattresses in each motel room was cost prohibitive for owners, so he retired to his basement "research facility" to refine his idea. He developed a portable model. The earliest units were far too big and shook violently. He finally came up with a much smaller version that could be used with existing mattresses and were coin-operated at 15 minutes for a quarter.

NEW AND IMPROVED

Franchisers sold the new models to motels for $45. After installation, the franchisers collected 80 percent of the revenue, and motel owners got the remaining 20 percent. The average haul for a week was $2 per room. Houghtaling sold a lot of franchises, and the monthly sales exceeded $2 million.

Eventually, the novelty of the units wore off, and motel owners found that guests were prying open the coin boxes and stealing the proceeds. Magic Fingers machines were discontinued, but you can still buy a home version of the gadget online.

SURE I MEANT TO INVENT THAT

PLAY-DOH

One smell most people remember from their childhood is the magical aroma of Play-Doh, the brightly colored, non-toxic modeling clay. Play-Doh was accidentally invented in 1955 by Joseph and Noah McVicker while they were trying to create a wallpaper cleaner. It was marketed a year later by toy manufacturer Rainbow Crafts. More than 900 million pounds of Play-Doh have been sold since then, but the recipe remains a secret.

FIREWORKS

Fireworks originated in China some 2,000 years ago, and legend has it that they were accidentally invented by a cook who mixed together charcoal, sulfur, and saltpeter—items commonly found in kitchens in those days. The mixture burned, and when compressed in a bamboo tube, it exploded. There's no record of whether it was the cook's last day on the job.

POTATO CHIPS

If you can't eat just one potato chip (and who can?), blame it on chef George Crum. He reportedly created the salty snack in 1853 at Moon's Lake House near Saratoga Springs, New York. Annoyed with a customer who continuously sent his fried potatoes back, complaining that they were soggy and not crunchy enough, Crum sliced the potatoes as thin as possible, fried them in hot grease, then doused them with salt. The customer loved them, and Crum's "Saratoga Chips" quickly became a must-have item at Moon's Lake House and throughout New England. Eventually, the chips were mass-produced for home consumption. However, since they were stored in barrels or tins, they quickly went stale. Then, in the 1920s, Laura Scudder invented the airtight bag by ironing together two pieces of waxed paper, thus keeping the chips fresh longer.

SACCHARIN

Saccharin is the oldest artificial sweetener. It was accidentally discovered in 1879 by researcher Constantine Fahlberg, who was working at Johns Hopkins University in the laboratory of professor Ira Remsen. Fahlberg's discovery came after he forgot to wash his hands before lunch. He had spilled a chemical on his hands, and it caused the bread he ate to taste unusually sweet. In 1880, the two scientists jointly published the discovery, but in 1884, Fahlberg obtained a patent and began mass-producing saccharin without Remsen. The use of saccharin did not become widespread until sugar was rationed during World War I, and its popularity increased during the 1960s and 1970s with the manufacture of Sweet'N Low and diet soft drinks.

POST-IT NOTES

A Post-it Note is a small piece of paper with a strip of low-tack adhesive on the back that allows it to temporarily be attached to documents, walls, computer monitors, and just about anyplace else. The idea for the Post-it Note was conceived in 1974 by Arthur Fry as a way of holding bookmarks in his hymnal while singing in the church choir. He was aware of an adhesive accidentally developed in 1968 by fellow 3M employee Spencer Silver. No application for the lightly sticky stuff had been apparent until Fry's inspiration. The 3M company was initially skeptical about the product's profitability, but in 1980, Post-it Notes were introduced nationally. Today, the sticky notes are sold in more than 100 countries.

DEADLY INVENTIONS

The success of history's most famous inventors rested not just upon brilliant ideas but also upon having the dedication and confidence to pursue those ideas in the face of public doubt. Unfortunately, inventors have sometimes been too confident in their work—with disastrous consequences.

HENRY WINSTANLEY, LIGHTHOUSE ARCHITECT

While 17th-century lighthouse-smith Henry Winstanley didn't invent the first lighthouse, he did design a brand new kind of lighthouse—the Eddystone Lighthouse. This octagonal-shaped structure was built to withstand treacherous conditions on unstable ground. Despite observers' doubts that his invention would stand up to any serious meteorological assault, Winstanley believed in his design—so much so that he insisted on taking shelter in it during a terrible storm in November 1703. It was a poor decision—the lighthouse collapsed, ending Winstanley's life.

MARIE CURIE, RADIATION PIONEER

Marie Curie is known to schoolchildren as the discoverer of the elements radium and polonium, the first woman to win a Nobel Prize, a pioneer in the field of radioactivity, and the inventor of a method for isolating radioactive isotopes. Unfortunately, she is also known as a pioneer in the field of radiation-induced cancer. Curie, who was working with radioactive isotopes well before the dangers of radiation were fully known, contracted leukemia from radiation exposure and died at age 66.

WILLIAM BULLOCK, INVENTOR OF THE WEB ROTARY PRINTING PRESS

Before the 19th century, the printing press hadn't advanced much beyond Gutenberg's first effort back in the 15th century. In 1863, William Bullock changed everything by coming up with the idea of a web rotary press—a self-feeding, high-speed press that could print as many as 10,000 pages per hour. Unfortunately, Bullock forgot a basic rule of printing presses: Don't stick your foot into the rotating gears. In 1867, Bullock got tangled up in his invention, severely injuring his foot. Gangrene set in, and he died shortly afterward.

KAREL SOUCEK, INVENTOR OF THE "STUNT CAPSULE"

Soucek hurtled to fame in 1984 by designing a special stunt capsule that he used to plunge over Niagara Falls. Seeking to capitalize on his newfound popularity, Soucek decided to repeat the stunt in 1985—only this time from an artificial waterfall running from the top of the Houston Astrodome down to a tank of water. If this seems like a bad idea, that's because it was: The capsule exploded upon impact, and Soucek suffered fatal injuries.

OTTO LILIENTHAL, INVENTOR OF THE HANG GLIDER

Until the late 19th century, human flight was little more than a pipe dream. Otto Lilienthal changed all of that with his hang glider, and his successful glides made him famous the world over. Unfortunately, in 1896, Lilienthal plunged more than 50 feet during one of his test runs. The fall broke his spine, and he died shortly after.

COWPER PHIPPS COLES, INVENTOR OF THE ROTATING SHIP TURRET

The splendidly named Cowper Phipps Coles was a captain in the British navy who invented a "rotating gun turret" for British naval vessels during the Crimean War. After the war, Coles patented his invention and set about building more ships equipped with his new turret.

Unfortunately, the first ship that he built, the HMS *Captain*, turned into the HMS Capsized. In order to accommodate his unusual turret design, the shipbuilders were forced to make odd adjustments to the rest of the ship, which seriously raised the center of gravity. End result? The ship sank on one of its first voyages, killing Coles and much of his crew.

A SHOCKING INVENTION: THE ELECTRIC CHAIR

Electrocution was meant to be a more humane form of execution, but things didn't exactly work out that way.

ALFRED SOUTHWICK'S LIGHTBULB MOMENT

Dr. Alfred Southwick was a dentist in Buffalo, New York, but he was no simple tooth-driller. Like many of his contemporaries in the Gilded Age of the 1870s and 1880s, he was a broad-minded man who kept abreast of the remarkable scientific developments of the day—like electricity. Though the phenomenon of electric current had been known of for some time, the technology of electricity was fresh—lightbulbs and other electric inventions had begun to be mass produced, and the infrastructure that brought electricity into the businesses and homes of the well-to-do was appearing in the largest cities.

So Southwick's ears perked up when he heard about a terrible accident involving this strange new technology. A man had walked up to one of Buffalo's recently installed generators and decided to see what all the fuss was about. In spite of the protests of the men who were working on the machinery, he touched something he shouldn't have and, to the shock of the onlookers, died instantly. Southwick pondered the situation with a cold, scientific intelligence and wondered if the instant and apparently painless death that high voltage had delivered could be put to good use.

Southwick's interest in electrocution wasn't entirely morbid. Death—or more specifically, execution—was much on people's minds in those days. Popular movements advocated doing away with executions entirely, while more moderate reformers simply wanted a new, more humane method of putting criminals to death. Hangings had fallen out of favor due to the potential for gruesome accidents, often caused by the incompetence of hangmen. While the hangman's goal was to break the criminal's neck instantly, a loose knot could result in an agonizingly slow suffocation; a knot that was too tight had the potential to rip a criminal's head clean off.

To prove the legitimacy of his idea, Southwick began conducting experiments on animals (you really don't want to know) and discussing the results with other scientists and inventors. He eventually published his work and attracted enough attention to earn himself an appointment on the Gerry Commission, which was created by the New York State Legislature in 1886 and tasked with finding the most humane method of execution.

Although the three-person commission investigated several alternatives, eventually it settled on electrocution—in part because Southwick had won the support of the most influential inventor of the day, Thomas Alva Edison, who had developed the incandescent lightbulb and was trying to build an empire of generators and wires to supply (and profit from) the juice that made his lightbulbs glow. Edison provided influential confirmation that an electric current could produce instant death; the legislature was convinced and a law that made electrocution the state's official method of execution was passed.

WILLIAM KEMMLER GETS ZAPPED

On August 6, 1890—after much technical debate (AC or DC? How many volts?) and a few experiments on animals (again, you don't want to know)—William Kemmler, an axe murderer, became the first convicted criminal to be electrocuted.

Southwick declared it a success, but the reporters who witnessed it felt otherwise. Kemmler had remained alive after the first jolt, foam was oozing from the mask that had been placed over his face as he struggled to breathe. A reporter fainted. A second jolt of several minutes was applied, and Kemmler's clothes and body caught fire. The stench of burned flesh was terrible.

Despite a public outcry, the state of New York remained committed to the electric method of execution. The technology and technique were improved, and eventually other states began to use electrocution as well. Today, nine states still allow use of the electric chair, though lethal injection is the preferred option.

STRANGE BUT TRUE INVENTIONS

PIERCED GLASSES

Tired of your glasses slipping down your nose? Try pierced glasses—spectacles that connect to a piercing surgically implanted into the nose. Invented by James Sooy in 2004, these glasses should appeal to body modification artists.

THE BULLETPROOF BED

Are you consumed with fearful thoughts when you go to bed? Perhaps you fear assassination? Strangling? Assault by zombies? Then maybe you'll rest more peacefully in a bulletproof bed. The Quantum Sleeper's coffin-like design protects from attacks, fires, and even some natural disasters with its airtight and waterproof interior. The bed features an air filtration system and can be fitted with DVD screens, a refrigerator, and even a microwave!

THE PORTABLE CROSSWALK

There never seems to be a crosswalk when you need one, and nobody wants to break the law by jaywalking. Instead, use a portable crosswalk, a vinyl sheet that can be spread across a busy street to ensure your safety as you make your way through traffic. Though its legality may be in question, it will certainly stop traffic . . . we hope.

SAUCE-DISPENSING CHOPSTICKS

Need to eliminate every bit of unproductive time from your busy daily schedule? Why not try sauce-dispensing chopsticks for the sushi eater in a rush? Now you will no longer have to waste valuable milliseconds dipping your food into an inconvenient container of soy sauce—just squeeze the end of the stick and the liquid flows right onto your food! The utensils can cost more than $20, but can you really put a price on time-savings of this magnitude?

THE DRYMOBILE

In this day and age, everyone is looking for new ways to save time and energy. Now you can do both with the Japanese Drymobile. Hang your clothes from a rack that fits conveniently on top of your car and your clothes will be dry in no time as you run your daily errands . . . unless, of course, it starts to rain.

ONE-CUT NAIL CLIPPERS

Staying well groomed can be quite time-consuming. But now at least one task can be shortened with one-cut nail clippers. A series of five clippers are positioned over the toes or fingernails, allowing the user to cut all five nails at once.

THE GAS GRABBER

Sometimes you just can't blame the dog. For those occasions, turn to the Gas Grabber, a charcoal filter that slips into your underwear to cover up those social faux pas. The filter was originally developed by the British to guard against nerve agents.

THE GRIN GRABBER

Some people just don't smile enough, so it's the Grin Grabber to the rescue! Attach a hook to each side of your mouth, grasp the string, and yank. The pulley system will lift the corners and soon you'll be beaming from ear to ear!

THE SNOT SUCKER

No tissue? No problem! The WIVA-VAC Nasal Aspirator uses vacuum power to clean up a runny nose. Perfect for children on the go, just slip the tapered end into a nostril and suck the snot right out of 'em!

THE DADDY NURSER

Since the beginning of time, men have been accused of not pulling their weight in the baby department. Now men can truly experience the joy of motherhood with the Daddy Nurser, a pair of milk-filled orbs that connect to a man's chest to mimic the act of breast-feeding. Now if they could only invent a way for men to give birth!

CHINDOGU

Chindogu is the perfect Japanese term for the items listed in the previous article. The word refers to the art of creating seemingly useful yet ultimately useless inventions—useless because no one would want to be seen with one in public. The classic example is the hay-fever hat, which consists of a roll of toilet paper secured to the head by a chinstrap. Another great example is the dumbbell phone, a free-weight attachment for the telephone that purportedly helps build muscle every time you pick up the handset. This works best if you have a lot of short conversations and, thus, are lifting the phone and setting it down every minute or so. (Perfect for telemarketers, perhaps?) There are (too many) others.

SNAKE OIL, WORM DIETS, AND GENERAL QUACKERY

> **PHRENOLOGY, n. The science of picking the pocket through the scalp. It consists in locating and exploiting the organ that one is a dupe with.**
> —Ambrose Bierce

From the love potions and elixirs of old times to the healing powers of New Age crystals, nowhere is human gullibility more apparent than in the tendency to seek out and believe in magical solutions to life's problems. Have you ever thought you were surrounded by mysterious energy sources? Welcome to a thriving club! In the 19th century, you may have enjoyed the healing magnetism of mesmerism. And the 20th century featured many shiny devices that allowed you to electrocute yourself into fitness and health. Today, why not enhance your biofield with energy medicine?

Or join us and follow the ley lines to the bank account for a closer look at the fakery behind the fads.

A HEADY HYPOTHESIS

Sure, someone may look like a nice enough guy, but a phrenologist might just diagnose the same fella as a potential axe murderer.

There are bumps in the road and bumps in life. Then there are the bumps on our heads. In the last half of the 19th century, the bumps and lumps and shapes of the human skull became an area of scientific study known as *phrenology*.

Early in the century, an Austrian physicist named Franz Joseph Gall theorized that the shape of the head followed the shape of the brain. Moreover, he wrote, the skull's shape was determined by the development of the brain's various parts. He described 27 separate parts of the brain and attributed to each one specific personality traits.

Gall's phrenological theories reached the public at a time of widespread optimism in Europe and North America. New and startling inventions seemed to appear every week. No problem was insurmountable, no hope unattainable. Physical science prevailed. By mid-century, Gall's theories had spread favorably throughout industrialized society. What was particularly attractive about phrenology was its value as both an indicator and predictor of psychological traits. If these traits could be identified—and phrenology presumably could do this—they could be re-engineered through "moral counseling" before they became entrenched as bad habits, which could result in socially unacceptable behavior. On the other hand, latent goodness, intellect, and rectitude could also be identified and nurtured.

As it grew in popularity, phrenology found its way into literature as diverse as the Brontë family's writings and those of Edgar Allen Poe. It also influenced the work of philosopher William James. Famed poet Walt Whitman was so proud of his phrenological chart that he published it five times. Thomas Edison was also a vocal supporter. "I never knew I had an inventive talent until phrenology told me so," he said. "I was a stranger to myself until then."

CRIMINAL MINDS

Early criminologists such as Cesare Lombroso and Èmile Durkheim (the latter considered to be the founder of the academic discipline of sociology) saw remarkable possibilities for phrenology's use in the study of criminal behavior. Indeed, according to one tale, the legendary Old West figure Bat Masterson invited a phrenologist to Dodge City to identify horse thieves and cattle rustlers. A lecture before an audience of gun-toting citizenry ended with the audience shooting out the lights and the lecturer hastily departing through the back exit.

In 1847, Orson Fowler, a leading American phrenologist, conducted an analysis of a Massachusetts wool trader and found him "to go the whole figure or nothing," a man who would "often find (his) motives are not understood." Sure enough, years later Fowler was proven to be on the money. The man was noted slavery abolitionist John Brown, and he definitely went the "whole figure."

BUMPOLOGY BOOMS

By the turn of the century, the famous and not so famous were flocking to have their skulls analyzed. Phrenology had become a fad and, like all fads, it attracted a number of charlatans. Death masks and cranial molds also became popular sideshow exhibits. By the 1920s, the science had degenerated into a parlor game. Disrepute and discredit followed, but not before new expressions slipped into the language. Among these: "lowbrow" and "highbrow" describe varying intellectual capacity, as well as the offhand remark, "You should have your head examined."

Nevertheless, phrenology did figure in the early development of American psychiatry, and it helped point medical scientists in new directions: neurology for one and, more recently, genomics—the study of the human genome.

FRANZ MESMER
TRANSFIXES EUROPE

The Age of Enlightenment saw the explosion of new ideas. One of these was the possibility of tapping into a person's subconscious, causing them to enter a dreamlike state where they might find relief from various ailments, whether through actual effect or merely by the power of a hypnotist's suggestion. One early practitioner of this technique became so famous that his very name became synonymous with the ability to send his patients into a trance—the art of mesmerism.

Franz Anton Mesmer was a late bloomer. Born in Germany in 1734, Mesmer had difficulty finding a direction in life. He first studied for the priesthood, then drifted into astronomy and law before finally graduating at age 32 from the University of Vienna with a degree in medicine. He set up practice in Vienna and married a well-to-do widow, becoming a doctor to the rich and famous and using his connections to cater to an upper-crust clientele. He lived comfortably on a Viennese estate and counted among his friends Wolfgang Amadeus Mozart, who wrote a piece for Mesmer to play on the glass harmonica, an instrument lately arrived from America.

At first, Mesmer's medical prescriptions were unremarkable; bleeding and purgatives were the order of the day, and Mesmer followed medical convention. But Mesmer's attention was also drawn to the practice of using magnets to induce responses in patients, a technique much in vogue at the time.

Mesmer experimented with magnets to some effect and came to believe that he was successfully manipulating tides, or energy flows, within the human body. He theorized that illness was caused by the disruption of these flows, and health could be restored by a practitioner who could put them back in order. He also decided that the magnets themselves were an unnecessary prop and that he was performing the manipulation of the tides himself, because of what he termed his animal magnetism—the word "animal" merely stemming from the Latin term for "breath" or "soul." He would stir the tides by sitting in a chair opposite a patient, knees touching, gazing unblinkingly into their eyes, making passes with his hands, and massaging the areas of complaint, often continuing the treatment for hours until the patient felt the magnetic flows moving inside their body.

EUROPE BECOMES MESMERIZED

Mesmer gained notoriety as a healer, his fame growing to the point where he was invited to give his opinion in other famous cases of the day. He investigated claims of unusual cures and traveled around Switzerland and Germany, holding demonstrations at which he was able to induce symptoms and their subsequent cures by merely pointing at people, much to the amazement of his audience. He also took on more challenging cases as a doctor, but a scandal involving his treatment of a blind piano player—he temporarily restored her sight, only to have her lose her audiences because the novelty of watching her play was now gone—caused Mesmer to decide that 1777 was an opportune year to move to Paris.

France would prove to be a fertile ground for Mesmer. He resumed seeing patients, while at the same time seeking approval from the scientific community of Paris for his techniques. The respect and acknowledgment he felt he deserved from his peers was never to come, but his popular reputation soared; Marie Antoinette herself wrote Mesmer and begged him to reconsider when he once announced that he intended to give up his practice. His services were in such demand that he could no longer treat patients individually; he resorted to treating groups of patients with a device he called a *baquet*, a wooden tub bristling with iron rods around which patients would hold hands and collectively seek to manipulate their magnetic tides. Mesmer himself would stride back and forth through the incense-laden room, reaching out and tapping patients with a staff or finger.

For a complete cure, Mesmer believed the patients needed to undergo a convulsive crisis—literally an experience wherein they would enter a trancelike state, shake and moan uncontrollably, and be carried to a special padded chamber until they had come back to their senses. The treatment proved particularly popular with women, who outnumbered men 8–1 as patients of Mesmer. This statistic did not go unnoticed by the monitors of public decency, who drew the obvious conclusion that something immoral was taking place, though they were unable to produce much more than innuendo in support of their accusations.

WHEN I SNAP MY FINGERS

Unfortunately, Mesmer's incredible popularity also made him an easy target for detractors. Mesmerism became such a fad that the wealthy even set up baquets in their own homes. But, as with many trends, once over they are held up for popular ridicule. As a result, Mesmer saw his client base decline and even found himself mocked in popular theater.

Copycats emerged to the extent that in 1784, the king set up a commission—including representatives from both the Faculty of Medicine and the Royal Academy of Science—to investigate all claims of healing involving animal magnetism. Benjamin Franklin, in Paris as an ambassador at the time, was one of the investigators. In the end, the commission determined that any treatment benefits derived from Mesmerism were imagined. This rejection by the scientific community combined with the erosion of his medical practice drove Mesmer from Paris in 1785. He kept an understandably low profile after that, spending some time in Switzerland, where he wrote and kept in touch with a few patients. He died in 1815.

The legitimacy of Mesmer's practice remains unresolved. Some still view him as a charlatan of the first order. Others see in his techniques the foundation of modern hypnotherapy, which has become a well-recognized practice in modern psychiatry. Regardless, it is indisputable that Franz Anton Mesmer's personal animal magnetism continues to capture our imagination even today.

EAT WORMS, LOSE WEIGHT!

No matter what anyone tells you, the only way to successfully lose weight is to eat less and exercise more. Yet this common-sense knowledge hasn't stopped millions from trying anything to make the road to weight loss smoother—including purposely ingesting parasites. Wouldn't it be easier to just go on a walk and skip dessert?

THOSE WACKY EARLY 1900s

There was a time not so long ago when cocaine was the cure for multiple ailments and smoking was considered an invigorating habit. So not many feathers were ruffled when ads showed up advertising a tapeworm pill for ladies looking to slim down. The ads, which first appeared between 1900 and 1920, claimed that by ingesting a pill containing tapeworm larvae, you could give a hungry worm a happy home and shed pounds like nobody's business. You could eat all you wanted, content in the knowledge that your new friend would be eating up most of the calories you consumed, thus allowing you to lose weight without thinking twice about it.

No one can prove that the pills advertised back then actually contained worm larvae. The pills could have been placebos, and for the foolish folks who tried the diet fad, we can only hope that's what they were.

THE WORM IS BACK!

The weight loss via tapeworm idea died down for many years (obesity was not as much of an issue during the Great Depression and both World Wars), but enthusiasm for it resurfaced in the 1960s. Rumors that the new appetite suppressant candy introduced to the market contained worm eggs started getting around, though of course, this was entirely false.

After a remarkable weight loss of an estimated 65 pounds, acclaimed opera star Maria Callas endured a round of heavy gossip that she had purposely acquired a tapeworm to do it. Though the singer indeed was diagnosed with a tapeworm, her doctor suggested it was due to her fondness for eating beef tartare. Other celebrities are rumored to have swallowed tapeworm pills to whittle down their figures, including model Claudia Schiffer, though this was never confirmed.

Search the Internet these days and you'll find a plethora of companies that advertise "sterile tapeworms" (whatever that means) for a variety of medicinal uses (whether they're selling a real product or scamming the public is another article). The fine print is lengthy, however, as using tapeworms to treat any condition has not been approved by the USDA. To get your worms, you'll likely have to go to Mexico. These stowaways will get you in big trouble if you try to bring them back across the U.S. border.

TAPEWORMS: NOT A GOOD PET

A lot of time and attention is spent around the world trying to keep worms from getting into the human body via water, food, or skin. Simply put, having a tapeworm is not a good thing. In the case of the fish tapeworm, especially, the essential vitamin B12 is sucked out of the host's body and depletes the vital ingredient for making red blood cells.

Adult tapeworms can grow up to 50 feet long and live up to 20 years. Depending on the worm, a host's symptoms range from epileptic seizures, diarrhea, nausea, fatigue, a swollen belly (oh, the irony), and even death. While it's likely a person with a worm will lose weight, they'll also suffer from malnutrition— B12 isn't the only nutrient eaten by the parasite. And tapeworm eggs are an inevitable byproduct of a tapeworm. The fish tapeworm can produce a million eggs in a single day, and the larvae tend to burrow out of the intestines and find homes elsewhere in the body, like the brain, for example. Worms also have the habit of popping out of various orifices without warning, too.

Still interested in tapeworms as a form of weight loss? Then perhaps it's your head, and not your pants size, that's the issue!

DON'T GET HYSTERICAL

Of all the strange medical diagnoses of yore, hysteria might be one of the strangest. Used frequently in the Victorian era, it eventually became one of the most common diagnoses in the history of Western medicine. Hysteria, particularly female hysteria, was a catchall for any kind of "woman problems" ladies might experience and was indicated by a long list of symptoms: fainting, anxiety, insomnia, muscle spasm, mood swings, loss of appetite, heaviness in abdomen, shortness of breath, retention of fluids, disinterest in sex, etc. In other words, if you were a woman who felt at all ill or were thought to be "acting up," you were probably just hysterical and needed to get a grip! How did doctors arrive at this diagnosis and what were the treatments? The history of hysteria will make you glad medicine has progressed since Victorian times.

ANCIENT ORIGINS AND INITIAL "CURES"

The word *hysteria* comes from the Greek word *hysterikos*, meaning "suffering of the womb." In fact, during ancient times, the uterus was thought to move around in the body, wreaking all kinds of havoc (e.g., strangling the woman and causing diseases). This phenomenon, first suggested by Aretaeus of Cappodocia, was known as the "wandering womb." According to the *Encyclopedia of Gender and Society*, physicians continued to believe in the wandering womb throughout the classical, medieval, and renaissance periods.

The ancient Greeks believed that women were actually "incomplete" males; thus, the uterus was not a cooperative organ: it was in rebellion against the female body. So the cure for hysteria was to resituate the uterus or "lure it back" via rocking in a chair, riding a horse, or receiving a "pelvic massage." It was recommended that married women have sexual intercourse with their husbands, while single women were encouraged to get married—pronto!

VICTORIAN HYSTERIA

In Victorian times, sex as a form of pleasure, rather than strictly a form of reproduction, was particularly taboo. Society upheld the notion of the "sexless woman." Therefore, almost any woman who deviated from this ideal or experienced sexual frustration or emotional turmoil was deemed hysterical. In fact, by the mid-19th century, physicians diagnosed a quarter of all women as hysterical. Meanwhile, the number of symptoms for this "disease" kept growing. One physician catalogued 75 pages of possible symptoms—a list he described as incomplete.

GOODBYE, LEECH CURES!

How to treat the hysterical masses? Doctors prescribed bed rest, seclusion, sensory deprivation, tasteless food, and pelvic massages (which basically brought about an orgasm). The latter were to be performed by a skilled physician or midwife and were often accompanied by a steady flow of water, otherwise known as a hydrotherapy treatment. The massage treatment eventually gave rise to the first electromechanical vibrator. Doctors also recommended that hysterical women stay away from any tasks that were too mentally strenuous, such as reading and writing. Of course, this sort of deprivation just created more problems. In *The Yellow Wallpaper*, the short story written by Charlotte Perkins Gilman in 1899, a woman is driven mad after being prescribed a "rest cure" for hysteria. She is locked in an upstairs room and denied any real form of social, physical, or mental activity. For Gilman, this turn of events hit close to home: She, too, was labeled "hysterical" and prescribed such a cure.

Some alternative remedies for female hysteria included prescribing cod liver oil or applying leeches to the cervix. In the early 20th century, the studies of Austrian psychiatrist Sigmund Freud supported the idea of a female sexual drive, so society eventually retreated from the idea of the "sexless woman."

By mid-century, there was a noticeable decline in the number of diagnoses, and eventually, the American Psychiatric Association omitted hysteria from the list of official medical conditions. Doctors favored more specific and accurate diagnoses, reclassifying patients as having post-partum depression, anxiety disorders, schizophrenia, or other forms of mental illness, rather than hysteria.

THE LOBOTOMY: A SORDID HISTORY

There's a reason why lobotomies have taken a place next to leeches in the Health Care Hall of Shame.

BEYOND HOLLYWOOD

Few people have firsthand experience with lobotomized patients. For many of us, any contact with these convalescents comes via Hollywood—that searing image at the end of *One Flew Over the Cuckoo's Nest* of Jack Nicholson, as Randle Patrick McMurphy, lying comatose. Hopefully, we've all experienced enough to know that Hollywood doesn't always tell it like it is. What would be the point of a medical procedure that turns the patient into a vegetable? Then again, even if Hollywood is prone to exaggeration, the fact is that a lobotomy is a pretty terrible thing.

DISSECTING THE LOBOTOMY

What exactly is a lobotomy? Simply put, it's a surgical procedure that severs the paths of communication between the prefrontal lobe and the rest of the brain. This prefrontal lobe—the part of the brain closest to the forehead—is a structure that appears to have great influence on personality and initiative. So the obvious question is: Who the heck thought it would be a good idea to disconnect it?

It started in 1890, when German researcher Friederich Golz removed portions of his dog's brain. He noticed afterward that the dog was slightly more mellow—and the lobotomy was born. The first lobotomies performed on humans took place in Switzerland two years later.

The six patients who were chosen all suffered from schizophrenia, and while some did show post-op improvement, two died. Apparently this was a time in medicine when an experimental procedure that killed 33 percent of its subjects was considered a success. Despite these results, lobotomies became more common, and one early proponent of the surgery even received a Nobel Prize.

The most notorious practitioner of the lobotomy was American physician Walter Freeman, who performed the procedure on more than three thousand patients— including Rosemary Kennedy, the sister of President John F. Kennedy—from the 1930s to the 1960s.

Freeman pioneered a surgical method in which a metal rod (known colloquially as an "ice pick") was inserted into the eye socket, driven up into the brain, and hammered home. This is known as a transorbital lobotomy.

Freeman and other doctors lobotomized about 40,000 patients before an outcry over the procedure prevailed in the 1950s. Although the mortality rate had improved since the early trials, it turned out that the ratio of success to failure was not much higher: A third of the patients got better, a third stayed the same, and a third became much worse. The practice had generally ceased in the United States by the early 1970s, and it is now illegal in some states.

WHO GOT THEM?

Lobotomies were performed only on patients with extreme psychological impairments, after no other treatment proved to be successful. The frontal lobe of the brain is involved in reasoning, emotion, and personality, and disconnecting it can have a powerful effect on a person's behavior. Unfortunately, the changes that lobotomies cause are unpredictable and often negative. Today, there are far more precise and far less destructive ways of affecting the brain through antipsychotic drugs and other pharmaceuticals.

So it's not impossible that Nicholson's character in *Cuckoo's Nest* could become zombie-like. If the movie gets anything wrong, it's that a person as highly functioning as McMurphy probably wouldn't have been recommended for a lobotomy. The vindictive Nurse Ratched is the one who makes the call, which raises a fundamental question: Who is qualified to decide whether someone should have a lobotomy?

GREAT ACHIEVEMENTS
IN MEDICAL FRAUD

If you were diagnosed at the turn of the century with lumbago, puking fever, black vomit, consumption, decrepitude, falling sickness, milk leg, ship fever, softening of the brain, St. Vitus's dance, trench mouth, dropsy, or heaven forbid, dyscrasy, then chances are you were in big trouble. Not only did the "modern" medical community misunderstand most of these diseases, they were also clueless as to how to treat them. This didn't prevent a cascade of creative cures, regimens, and health devices from being pedaled across the country.

Facing a life of interminable pain and suffering, many sufferers of these diseases resorted to the hundreds of unfounded medical treatments, which sometimes worked, sometimes didn't, and sometimes produced an obvious placebo effect. Here's a brief list of some of the more popular medical treatments and the claims by their originators:

- **The Battle Creek Vibratory Chair:** Many people who enjoy a hearty bowl of Corn Flakes in the morning are familiar with their inventor, Dr. John Harvey Kellogg of Battle Creek, Michigan. Dr. Kellogg also designed a number of intriguing therapeutic devices, including the Battle Creek Vibratory Chair. After the suffering patient was strapped in, the chair would shake them violently to "stimulate intestinal peristalsis" that was beneficial to digestive disorders. Prolonged vibratory chair treatments were also recommended to cure a variety of maladies from headaches to back pain.

- **The Toftness Radiation Detector:** If the Toftness Radiation Detector looks suspiciously like the PVC piping found at a hardware store, that's because it is. By passing PVC tubing outfitted with inexpensive lenses over the patient's back, chiropractors listened for a high-pitched "squeak" that meant that the device had detected areas of neurological stress, characterized by high levels of radiation. The device was widely used until 1984 when it was deemed worthless by the Food and Drug Administration.

- **The Foot-Operated Breast Enlarger Pump:** In the mid-1970s, silicone breast implant technology was still in its infancy. Instead, many women pining for larger breasts spent $9.95 for a foot-operated vacuum pump and a series of cups that promised "larger, firmer and more shapely breasts in only 8 weeks." As it turned out, more than four million women were duped into buying a device that produced nothing more than bruising.

- **The Crystaldyne Pain Reliever:** In 1996, one of the most popular pain relievers on the market was nothing more than a gas grill igniter. When the sufferer pushed on the plunger, the device sent a short burst of sparks and electrical shocks through the skin to cure headaches, stress, arthritis, menstrual cramps, earaches, flu, and nosebleeds. After being subjected to FDA regulations, however, the company disappeared with thousands of dollars, falsely telling their consumers that "their devices were in the mail."

- **The Prostate Gland Warmer and The Recto Rotor:** Even someone without the slightest bit of imagination would cringe at the idea of inserting a 4 1/2-inch probe connected to a 9-foot electrical cord into their rectum. However, for thousands of adventurous consumers in the 1910s, the Prostate Gland Warmer (featuring a blue lightbulb that would light up when plugged in) and the Recto Rotor promised the latest in quick relief from prostate problems, constipation, and piles.

- **The Radium Ore Revigator:** In 1925, thousands of unknowing consumers plunked down their hard-earned cash for a clay jar with walls that were impregnated with low-grade radioactive ore. The radioactive material was nothing more than that found in the dial of an inexpensive wristwatch, but the Revigator still promised to invigorate "tired" or "wilted" water that was put into it—"the cause of illness in one hundred and nine million out of the hundred and ten million people of the United States."

-

- **Hall's Hair Renewer:** For as long as there's been hair loss, there have been hair-loss cures. One of the better-known snake oils in the 19th century was Hall's Vegetable Sicilian Hair Renewer, which Reuben P. Hall began selling in 1894. According to the inventor, an Italian sailor passed the recipe on to him; the results promised hair growth and decreased grayness. The first version was composed of water, glycerine, lead sugar, and traces of sulfer, sage, raspberry leaves, tea, and oil of citronella. Eventually, the formula was adjusted to include two kinds of rum and trace amounts of lead and salt. Of course, lead is poisonous, and the ingredients had to be changed once again. Still, the product sold into the 1930s, perhaps because of its promise that "As a dressing it keeps the hair lustrous, soft and silken, and easy to arrange. Merit wins."

- **The Relaxacisor:** For anyone who hated to exercise but still wanted a lithe, athletic body, the Relaxacisor was the answer. Produced in the early 1970s, the Relaxacisor came with four adhesive pads that were applied to the skin and connected by electrodes to a control panel. The device would deliver a series of electrical jolts to the body, "taking the place of regular exercise" while the user reclined on a sofa. All 400,000 devices were recalled for putting consumers at risk for miscarriages, hernias, ulcers, varicose veins, epilepsy, and exacerbating preexisting medical conditions.

- **The Timely Warning:** In 1888, one of the most embarrassing and debilitating experiences a man could endure was an "amorous dream" or "night emission." Fortunately, Dr. E. B. Foote came up with the "Timely Warning," a circular, aluminum ring that was worn to prevent "the loss of the most vital fluids of the system— those secreted by the testicular glands." For better or for worse, no diagrams have been found to illustrate exactly just *how* the device was worn.

WHAT'S NEW IN VOODOO?

New Orleans is famous for many things, one of them being the voodoo shops competing to sell you a spell or two. Not surprisingly, New Orleans boasts at least four shops that specialize in every kind of voodoo paraphernalia, along with an honest-to-goodness voodoo museum. Its Creole heritage provides some qualification for New Orleans to bill itself as the voodoo capital of the world. Whether you're a believer in spells, love potions, mojos, and zombies or not, the items carried by these quaint shops are well worth the visit. It's an opportunity to inhale the essence that makes New Orleans unique among American cities.

DETAILS, DETAILS

The word *voodoo* is derived from the Fon word *voudoun* (spirit). Erzulie's, Bloody Mary's, Reverend Zombie's, and Voodoo Authentica are all voodoo shops located in the famed French Quarter of New Orleans. These shops offer a variety of items unique to the uninitiated, such as potion oils, gris-gris (lucky mojo bags), voodoo dolls, jujus (blessed objects that ward off evil), ritual kits (everything you need to perform your own voodoo ritual for less than $50), voodoo candles, handmade crafts, incense, jewelry (including chicken-foot fetishes and gator-tooth necklaces), voodoo spells, spiritual guidance, African power dolls, T-shirts, and much more.

You can even have a hex removed if someone was mean enough to lay one on you, or join a class to learn how to make your own voodoo doll.

Most of the shops also feature ghostly tours, which usually include a visit to the grave of Marie Laveau, one of the world's better-known voodoo queens and a popular woman in New Orleans history. So, the next time you're in New Orleans, don't be a zombie—drop into one of the city's unique voodoo shops and visit for a spell, especially during Voodoo Fest, which takes place every Halloween.

MILLIONS OF MUMMIES

*It sounds like the premise of a horror movie–
generation after generation of excess mummies just
piling up. But for the Egyptians, this was simply an
excuse to get a little creative.*

The ancient Egyptians took death seriously. Their culture
believed that the afterlife was a dark and tumultuous place
where departed souls (*ka*) needed protection throughout
eternity. By preserving their bodies as mummies, Egyptians
provided their souls with a resting place—without which they
would wander the afterlife forever.

Starting roughly around 3000 BC, Egyptian morticians began
making a healthy business on the mummy trade. On receiving
a corpse, they would first remove the brain and internal
organs and store them in jars. Next, they would stuff the body
with straw to maintain its shape, cover it in salt and oils to
preserve it from rotting, and then wrap it in linens—a
process that could take up to 70 days. Finally, the finished
mummies would be placed in decorated sarcophagi,
now ready to face eternity.

At first, mummification was so costly it remained the exclusive
domain of the wealthy, usually royalty. However, when the
middle class began adopting the procedure, the mummy
population exploded. Soon people were mummifying
everything—even crocodiles. The practice of mummifying the
family cat was also common; the owners saw it as an offering
to the cat goddess Bast.

Even those who could not afford to properly mummify their loved ones unknowingly contributed to the growing number of mummies. These folks buried their deceased relatives in the Egyptian desert, where the hot, arid conditions dried out the bodies and created an army of natural mummies. When you consider that this burial art was in use for more than 3,000 years, it's not surprising that over time the bodies began piling up—literally.

So, with millions of mummies lying around, local entrepreneurs began looking for ways to cash in on these buried treasures. To them, mummies were a natural resource, not unlike oil, which could be extracted from the ground and sold at a handsome profit to eager buyers around the world.

MUMMY MEDICINE

In medieval times, Egyptians began touting mummies for their secret medicinal qualities. European doctors began importing mummies, boiling off their oils and prescribing it to patients. The oil was used to treat a variety of disorders, including sore throats, coughs, epilepsy, poisoning, and skin disorders. Contemporary apothecaries also got into the act, marketing pulverized mummies to noblemen as a cure for nausea.

The medical establishment wasn't completely sold on the beneficial aspects of mummy medicine, however. Several doctors voiced their opinions against the practice, one writing that: "It ought to be rejected as loathsome and offensive," and another claiming: "This wicked kind of drugge doth nothing to help the diseased." A cholera epidemic, which broke out in Europe, was blamed on mummy bandages, and the use of mummy medicine was soon abandoned.

MUMMY MYTHS

There are so many stories regarding the uses of mummies that it's often hard to separate fact from fiction. Some historians suggest the linens that comprised mummy wrappings were used by 19th-century American and Canadian industrialists to manufacture paper. At the time, there was a huge demand for paper, and suppliers often ran short of cotton rags—a key ingredient in the paper-making process. Although there's no concrete proof, some historians claim that when paper manufacturers ran out of rags, they imported mummies to use in their place.

Another curious claim comes courtesy of Mark Twain. He wrote: "The fuel [Egyptian train operators] use for the locomotive is composed of mummies three thousand years old, purchased by the ton or by the graveyard for that purpose." This item, almost assuredly meant as satire, was taken as fact by readers of the day. However, there is no historical record of Egyptian trains running on burnt mummies. Besides, the mischievous Twain was never one to let a few facts get in the way of a good story. Perhaps those who believe the humorist's outlandish claim might offset it with another of his famous quotes: "A lie can travel halfway around the world while the truth is putting on its shoes."

IT HAD GLOWING EYES

**Believe nothing you hear,
and only one half that you see.**

—Edgar Allan Poe

Poe would know. After all, he was conspicuous
for goading his otherwise well-adjusted, outdoorsy
countrymen to think about *creepy things*—locked rooms,
mysterious assailants, thumping hallucinations, and all-
around macabre mental states. But his point, when it
comes to human reliability, is well taken.

There's a neat euphemism for the grist that makes up
cryptozoology, paranormal studies, and related fields.
It's called the "witness account." For some reason,
homespun, rambling narratives have a way of smoothing
over the doubts we may otherwise harbor about accounts
of backwoods encounters under poor lighting conditions.
Also helpful: blurry footage, illegible documents, and
references to shadowy government agencies. Noticeably
absent should be phrases like "when I finished the bottle,"
"insane side of the family," and "make some cash off this."

THINGS THAT GET MADE UP IN THE NIGHT: THE AMITYVILLE HOAX

The famous haunted house that has inspired books, movies, sequels, and remakes was nothing more than a successful fraud.

The story behind the myth of *The Amityville Horror* is as fascinating as the supposedly "true" events that spawned a best-selling book, a hit horror movie (and its sequels), and a 2005 remake. The adage "Never let the truth get in the way of a good story" could have been coined specifically for *The Amityville Horror*.

On November 13, 1974, six members of the DeFeo family were shot in their home in Amityville, New York. The sole remaining family member, Ronald "Butch" DeFeo, Jr., later confessed to killing his parents and siblings and was sentenced to 25 years to life. A year after the murders, George and Kathy Lutz, along with their three children, moved into the DeFeo house but stayed only 28 days, alleging the residence was possessed by demonic forces.

A New York TV station employed the services of a team of psychics and ghost hunters who duly confirmed the Lutzes' claims: The house was haunted. *The Amityville Horror: A True Story*, written by Jay Anson, was published in 1977 and became a national best seller; the movie was released in 1979.

Eventually, though, the truth began to emerge. Anson confessed that his book was based on tape-recorded recollections from the Lutzes and that he hadn't verified any facts. Furthermore, the Lutzes had never contacted the Amityville police department about mysterious activity. Weather records show that there was no snowfall on the day the family claimed to have discovered cloven hoofprints in the snow. Most damning of all was Butch DeFeo's attorney, who admitted that he and the Lutzes, inspired in part by the popular movie *The Exorcist*, had created the stories while drinking several bottles of wine.

BIGFOOT

Let's face it—if you had to pick one monster that stands head (and feet) above all others, it would be Bigfoot. Not only is it the stuff of legends, but its likeness has also been used to promote everything from pizza to beef jerky.

EARLY SIGHTINGS

Folktales from Native American tribes throughout the Northwest, the area that Bigfoot traditionally calls home, are filled with references to giant, apelike creatures roaming the woods. They described the beast as between seven and ten feet tall and covered in brown or dark hair. (Sasquatch, a common term used for the big-footed beast, is actually an anglicization of a Native American term for a giant supernatural creature.)

Walking on two legs, there was something human-like about Sasquatch's appearance, although its facial features more closely resembled those of an ape, and it had almost no neck. With looks like that, it's not surprising that Native American folklore often described the creature as cannibalistic, supernatural, and dangerous. Other tales, however, said Sasquatch appeared to be frightened of humans and mostly kept to itself.

It wasn't until the 1900s, when more and more woodlands were being devoured in the name of progress, that Sasquatch sightings started to increase. It was believed that, though generally docile, the beast did have a mean streak when feeling threatened. In July 1924, Fred Beck and several others were mining in a mountainous area of Washington State. One evening, the group spotted and shot at what appeared to be an apelike creature. After fleeing to their cabin, the group was startled when several more hairy giants began banging on the walls, windows, and doors. For several hours, the creatures pummeled the cabin and threw large rocks at it before disappearing shortly before dawn. After several such encounters in the same general vicinity, the area was renamed Ape Canyon.

MY, WHAT BIG FEET YOU HAVE!

In August 1958, Jerry Crew, a bulldozer operator, showed up for work at a wooded site in Bluff Creek, California. Walking up to his bulldozer, which had been left there overnight, Crew found giant footprints in the dirt. At first, they appeared to be the naked footprints of a man, but there was one major difference—these feet were huge! After the tracks appeared on several occasions, Crew took a cast of one of them and brought it to *The Humboldt Times* in Eureka, California. The following day, the newspaper ran a front-page story, complete with photos of the footprint and a name for the creature: Bigfoot. The story and photographs hit the Associated Press, and the name stuck.

Even so, the event is still rife with controversy. Skeptics claim that it was Ray Wallace, not Bigfoot, who made the tracks as a practical joke on his brother Wilbur, who was Crew's supervisor. Apparently the joke backfired when Crew arrived at the site first and saw the prints before Wilbur. However, Ray Wallace never admitted to faking the tracks or having anything to do with perpetrating a hoax.

VIDEO EVIDENCE?

In 1967, in response to numerous Bigfoot sightings in northern California, Roger Patterson rented a 16mm video camera in hopes of shooting footage of the elusive creature. Patterson and his friend, Robert Gimlin, spent several days on horseback traveling though the Six Rivers National Forest without coming across as much as a footprint.

Then, on October 20, the pair rounded a bend and noticed something dark and hairy crouched near the water. When the creature stood up on two legs and presented itself in all its hairy, seven-foot glory, that's when Patterson said he knew for sure he was looking at Bigfoot. Unfortunately, Patterson's horse saw the creature, too, and suddenly reared up. Because of this, it took Patterson several precious seconds to get off the horse and pull the video camera out of his saddlebag. Once he did that, he jogged toward the creature, filming as he went.

As the creature walked away, Patterson continued filming until his tape ran out. He quickly changed his film, and then both men retrieved their frightened horses and attempted to follow Bigfoot further before eventually losing sight of it.

When they arrived back in town, Patterson reviewed the film. Even though it was less than a minute long and extremely shaky in spots, the film appeared to show Bigfoot running away while occasionally looking toward the camera.

For most Bigfoot enthusiasts, the Patterson–Gimlin film stands as the Holy Grail of Bigfoot sightings—physical proof captured on video. Skeptics, however, alleged that Patterson and Gimlin faked the entire incident and filmed a man in an expensive monkey suit. Nevertheless, more than 40 years after the event occurred, the Patterson–Gimlin film is still one of the most talked about pieces of Bigfoot evidence, mainly because neither man ever admitted to a hoax and the fact that no one has been able to figure out how they faked it.

GONE SASQUATCHING

The fact that some people doubt the existence of Bigfoot hasn't stopped thousands of people from heading into the woods to try to find one. Even today, the hairy creature makes brief appearances here and there. Of course, sites like YouTube have given rise to dozens of "authentic" videos of Bigfoot, some of which are quite entertaining. Still, every once in a while, a video that deserves a second look pops up. For example, in 2005, ferry operator Bobby Clarke filmed almost three minutes of video of a Bigfoot-like creature on the banks of the Nelson River in Manitoba.

THE PHILIP PHENOMENON: CREATING A GHOST OUT OF THIN AIR

Which came first: the phantom or the séance?
That's the million-dollar question regarding the
Philip Phenomenon—an astonishing experiment that
successfully conjured up a spirit. The only problem is
that this ghost never really lived. Or did it?

It all began in 1972, when members of the Toronto Society for Psychical Research (TSPR) conducted an experiment to determine if they could "create" a ghost and study how the power of suggestion affected the results. They wanted to know if they could work with a totally fictitious character—a man they invented from scratch—and somehow make contact with its spirit. And they did.

Dr. A.R.G. Owen, the organization's chief parapsychology researcher, gathered a group of eight people who were interested in the paranormal but had no psychic abilities of their own. The Owen Group, as it was called, was made up of people from all walks of life, including Owen's wife, an accountant, an industrial designer, a former MENSA chairwoman, a housewife, a student, and a bookkeeper. Dr. Joel Whitton, a psychologist, was also present at many of the meetings as an observer.

THE MAKING OF A GHOST

The first order of business was to create the ghost, giving it physical characteristics and a complete background story.

According to Dr. Owen, it was important to the study that the spirit be a total work of fiction, with no strong ties to any historical figure.

The group named the ghost Philip and proceeded to bring him to life—on paper, that is. A sketch artist even drew a picture of Philip as the group imagined him. Here is his story:

Philip Aylesford was an aristocratic Englishman who was born in 1624. As a supporter of the King, he was knighted at age 16 and went on to make a name for himself in the military. He married Dorothea, the beautiful daughter of a nobleman who lived nearby. Unfortunately, Dorothea's appearance was deceiving, as her personality was cold and unyielding. As a Catholic, Philip wouldn't divorce his wife, so he found escape by riding around the grounds of his estate. One day, he came across a gypsy camp. There, he found true love in the arms of the raven-haired Margo, whose dark eyes seemed to look into his soul. He brought her to Diddington Manor, his family home, and hid her in the gatehouse near the stable. But it wasn't meant to be: Dorothea soon discovered her husband's secret affair and retaliated by accusing the gypsy woman of stealing and practicing witchcraft. Afraid of damaging his own reputation, Philip did not step forward in Margo's defense, and she was burned at the stake. After the death of his beloved, Philip was tormented with guilt and loneliness; he killed himself in 1654 at age 30.

FOCUS, FOCUS, FOCUS

In September 1972, after the tale was written, the group began meeting regularly. Reports of these meetings vary.

Some accounts describe them as mere gatherings in which group members would discuss Philip and meditate on the details of his life. With no results after about a year, the group moved on to a more traditional method of communing with ghosts: holding séances in a darkened room, sitting around a table with appropriate music and objects that might have been used by Philip or his family. Another version has the group beginning with séances and switching to the more casual setting later. The setting itself is ultimately secondary to the results: Through the focus and concentration of the group, Philip soon began to make his presence known. He answered questions by tapping on the table for "yes" or "no." Just to be sure, a "yes" tap confirmed that he was, indeed, Philip.

A PHYSICAL PRESENCE

After communication was established, the Philip Phenomenon took on a life of its own. Through the tapping, Philip was able to answer questions about the details of his life. He was also able to correctly answer questions about people and places of that historical time period, although these were all facts that were familiar to at least one member of the group. Philip even seemed to develop a personality, exuding emotions that changed the atmosphere of the entire room. But most amazingly, he was able to exhibit some remarkable physical manifestations, such as making objects move, turning lights on and off at the group's request, and performing incredible feats with the table: It shifted, it danced on one leg, and it even moved across the room.

In order to demonstrate the results of this experiment, the group held a séance in front of an audience of 50 people; the session was also videotaped. Philip rose to the occasion—

and so did the table. In addition to tapping on the table and manipulating the lights, Philip made the entire table levitate half an inch off the ground!

The experiment was deemed a success, as there was little doubt that something paranormal was occurring during the sessions. However, the Owen Group never actually realized its original goal of getting the ghost of Philip to materialize. But the TSPR did go on to re-create the experiment successfully on several other occasions with a new group and a new fictional "ghost."

REAL, RANDOM, OR RE-CREATION?

So what can be concluded from all this? No one knows for sure, but several schools of thought have developed regarding the matter. Some believe that Philip was a real ghost and that he had once been a living, breathing person. Perhaps he had a few of the characteristics of the fictional Philip and simply responded to the group's summons. Some who believe in the ghost theory say that it may have been a playful spirit (or a demonic one) that just pretended to be Philip as a prank.

A less-popular theory suggests that someone close to the group was aware of the background information as well as the times and places of the meetings. He or she might have planned an elaborate hoax to make it appear as though the ghost was real.

But it is also possible that after creating Philip, the Owen Group put forth enough energy, focus, and concentration to bring him to life, in a manner of speaking. Ghosts may well be products of our imaginations, existing only in our minds, but this study does prove one thing: When people put those minds together, anything is possible—even a visit from the Other Side.

THE MYSTERY OF THE LOVELAND FROG

If anyone ever runs into a four-foot-tall human-like creature with a frog's face and webbed feet, for the love of Kermit, take a picture. The legend of the Loveland Frog dates back decades—yet, like so many other unusual creatures in American folklore, no firm evidence of its existence has ever been found.

The Loveland Frog was supposedly spotted in the town of Loveland, Ohio (hence the name). As the story goes, chatter of the leathery-skinned croaker first came up when French explorers began colonizing the region. Indians native to the area warned the pioneers about the immortal beast they called "Shawnahooc," or "demon of the river."

Actual sightings were not reported until the mid-1950s. That's when, in May 1955, someone reported seeing three frog-people just chilling on a bridge over the Little Miami River. One was said to be carrying some sort of bar that was sending off blue sparks. The observer, a local businessman, noted that the creatures' chests were lopsided, their lips froglike, and their scent a mix of alfalfa and almonds. Sounds lovely, eh?

The Loveland Frog's next alleged appearance came in 1972, when a police officer named Ray Shockey said he spotted a diminutive person with a froggy face sitting on a guardrail in the same vicinity. Two weeks later, another officer, Mark Matthews, was said to have seen the same thing lying in the road. Of course, when the officer tried to approach it (and shoot it), Mr. L. F. leapt into the river, never to be seen again.

LEGACY IN LOVELAND

The Loveland Frog may not have been seen in a while, but its tall tale lives on among the locals in the clearly action-packed town of Loveland. One man told a local newspaper he and his friends spent entire summers searching for signs of the amphibian hybrid. "For the whole summer in 1972, me and my friends, we went through the river at night with frog gigs and shotguns, looking for the thing," he said. "Every now and then, we seen something across the river. All we managed to catch, though, were redhorse suckers." (Redhorse suckers are sucker fish with red-tinted fins.)

FACT OR FICTION?

So is the Loveland Frog real, or is it little more than misguided myth? It all depends on whom you ask. Mark Matthews, the second officer who supposedly spotted the beast, told *X-Project Paranormal Magazine* in 2001 that the reports had been greatly exaggerated over the years. "There is absolutely nothing to the incident that relates to 'monsters' or the 'paranormal,'" he said. "This entire thing has been habitually blown out of proportion."

According to Matthews's interview, the Loveland Frog was not a monster, wasn't leathery, and didn't even stand on two feet. Rather, Matthews clarifies, the animal was some sort of lizard that likely escaped from somewhere nearby. "It was less than 3 feet in length, ran across the road, and was probably blinded by my headlights. It presented no aggressive action," he said.

IT CAME FROM . . . THE USA

MOMO

In the early 1970s, reports came flooding in of a strange creature inhabiting the woods near the small town of Louisiana, Missouri. Standing nearly seven feet tall, Momo (short for Missouri Monster) was completely covered in a blackish fur and had glowing orange eyes. The first major report came in July 1971 when Joan Mills and Mary Ryan claimed to have been harassed by a "half ape, half man" creature that made bizarre noises at them as they passed it on Highway 79. Even though the creature didn't make physical contact with them, both women believed it would have harmed them had it been given the chance.

That seemed to be confirmed the following year when, on July 11, 1972, brothers Terry and Wally Harrison spotted a giant, hairy beast carrying a dead dog. The boys screamed, alerting family members, who caught a glimpse of the creature before it disappeared into the woods. Sightings continued for a couple of weeks, but Momo hasn't been seen since.

DOVER DEMON

For two days in 1977, the town of Dover, Massachusetts, was under attack from a bizarre creature that seemed to be from another world. The first encounter with the beast— nicknamed the Dover Demon—occurred on the evening of April 21. Bill Bartlett was out for a drive with some friends when they saw something strange climbing on a stone wall. The creature appeared to be only about three feet tall but had a giant, oversize head with large, orange eyes. The rest of the body was tan and hairless with long, thin arms and legs.

Several hours later, the same creature was spotted by 15-year-old John Baxter, who watched it scurry up a hillside. The following day, a couple reported seeing the Demon, too. When authorities asked for a description, the couple's matched the ones given by the other witnesses except for one difference: The creature the couple encountered appeared to have glowing green eyes. Despite repeated attempts to locate it, the creature was never seen again.

LAWNDALE THUNDERBIRD

If you're ever in Lawndale, Illinois, keep an eye out for giant birds lest they sneak up on you and whisk you away. That's what almost happened in 1977 when Lawndale residents noticed two large black birds with white-banded necks and 10- to 12-foot wingspans flying overhead. The birds, though enormous, seemed harmless enough. That is, until they swooped down and one of them reportedly tried to take off with ten-year-old Marlon Lowe while he played in his yard. The boy was not seriously injured, but the thunderbird did manage to lift the terrified boy several feet off the ground and carry him for nearly 40 feet before dropping him. Over the next few weeks, the birds were seen flying over various houses and fields in nearby towns, but, thankfully, they did not attack anyone else.

GATORMEN

The swamplands of Florida are filled with alligators, but most of them don't have human faces. Since the 1700s, tales of strange half-man, half-alligator creatures have circulated throughout the area. Gatormen are described as having the face, neck, chest, and arms of a man and the midsection, back legs, and tail of an alligator. Unlike most other monsters and strange beasts, Gatormen reportedly prefer to travel and hunt in packs and even appear to have their own verbal language. What's more, recent sightings have them traveling outside the state of Florida and taking up residence in the swamplands of Louisiana and swimming around a remote Texas swamp in 2001.

SKUNK APE

Since the 1960s, a creature has been spotted in the Florida Everglades that many call Bigfoot's stinky cousin: the skunk ape. The beast is said to closely resemble Bigfoot with one minor difference—it smells like rotten eggs. In late 2000, Sarasota police received an anonymous letter from a woman who complained that an escaped animal was roaming near her home at night. Included with the letter were two close-up photographs of the creature—a large beast that resembled an orangutan standing behind some palmetto leaves, baring its teeth.

OHIO BRIDGE TROLLS

In May 1955, a man driving along the Miami River near Loveland, Ohio, came across a frightening sight. Huddled under a darkened bridge were several bald-headed creatures, each three to four feet tall. Spellbound, the man pulled over and watched the creatures, which he said had webbed hands and feet.

Though they made no sound, the man said the weird beings appeared to be communicating with each other and did not acknowledge him watching them. However, when one of the creatures held up a wand or rod that began emitting showers of sparks, the man quickly left. He drove straight to the local police station, which dispatched a car to the bridge. A search of the area turned up nothing, and, to this day, there have been no more reported sightings of these mysterious creatures.

MARYLAND'S GOATMAN

Think goats are cute and fuzzy little creatures? If so, a trip through Prince George's County in Maryland just might change your mind. Since the 1950s, people have reported horrifying encounters with a creature known only as the Goatman. From afar, many claim to have mistaken the Goatman for a human being. But as he draws nearer, his cloven feet become visible, as do the horns growing out of his head. If that's not enough to make you turn and run, reports as recent as 2006 state that the Goatman now carries an ax with him.

DEVIL MONKEYS

Far and away, some of the strangest creatures said to be roaming the countryside are the Devil Monkeys. Take an adult kangaroo, stick a monkey or baboon head on top, and you've got yourself a Devil Monkey. By most accounts, these creatures can cover hundreds of feet in just a few quick hops. They're nothing to tangle with, either. Although Devil Monkeys have traditionally stuck to attacking livestock and the occasional family pet, some reports have them attempting to claw their way into people's homes. Originally spotted in Virginia in the 1950s, Devil Monkeys have now been spotted all across the United States. On a related note, in May 2001, residents of New Delhi, India, were sent into a panic when a four-foot-tall half-monkey, half-human creature began attacking them as they slept.

A TALE IN NEED OF EXORCISING

The Exorcist was based on a story—that much is certain.

In January 1949, a 13-year-old boy named Roland (some sources say that his name was Robbie) and his family—who lived in Mount Rainier, Maryland—began hearing scratching sounds from behind the walls and inside the ceiling of their house. Believing that their home was infested with mice, Roland's parents called an exterminator. However, the exterminator found no evidence of rodents in the house. After that, the family's problem got a little worse: They began to hear unexplained footsteps in the home, and objects such as dishes and furniture seemed to relocate on their own.

But these incidents would seem minor compared to what came next: Roland claimed that an invisible entity attacked him and that his bed shook so violently that he couldn't sleep. The sheets and blankets were repeatedly ripped from his bed and tossed onto the floor. One time, Roland tried to grab them, but he was yanked onto the floor with the bedcovers still clenched in his fists.

Roland liked board games, and his aunt "Tillie"—a woman who had a strong interest in the supernatural—had taught him how to use a Ouija board before she died. Some blamed the Ouija board for causing the trouble, claiming that it had allowed a demonic being to come into the home and target Roland.

NOT SUCH GOOD VIBRATIONS

By this time, the family was convinced that some kind of evil entity had moved into their home, so they appealed to a Lutheran minister named Schulze for help. Reverend Schulze prayed for Roland and had his entire congregation do so as well. He even took Roland to his own home so the boy could get some sleep. However, both the bed and an armchair that Roland tried to sleep in there vibrated, shook, and moved around, allowing the boy no rest. Schulze noted that Roland seemed to go into a trance while these incidents occurred.

If Schulze had any doubt that it was time to call in the cavalry, he was certainly convinced when scratches mysteriously materialized on Roland's body. These scratches were then replaced by words that appeared to be made by claws. The word *Louis* was clearly visible,

which for some reason was interpreted as St. Louis—
Roland's mother's hometown. With all signs pointing to the
need for an exorcism, Father Edward Albert Hughes of St.
James Catholic Church was summoned.

TRUTH OR FICTION?

At this point, accounts of the story begin to splinter, as no
two versions are alike. According to the version that has
been more or less accepted as fact, Father Hughes went to
see Roland and was disturbed when the boy addressed him
in Latin—a language that was unknown to the youth.

Hughes decided to perform an exorcism, during which a
loose bedspring slashed him. The priest was supposedly
so shaken by the ordeal that he was never the same again.
(However, according to some sources, this part of the
story never happened; they say that Hughes only saw
Roland once at St. James, Roland never spoke in Latin, and
Hughes never performed an exorcism on the boy, nor was
he physically or emotionally affected by it. It is unclear why
someone felt that dramatic license needed to be taken here.)

During Roland's visit to Hughes, the priest suggested
using blessed candles and special prayers to help the boy.
But when Roland's mother did this, a comb flew across
the room, hitting the candles and snuffing them out. Other
objects also flew around the room, and at one point, a Bible
was thrown at the boy's feet. Supposedly, Roland had to
stop attending school because his desk shook so badly.

It seems that an attempt was made to baptize Roland into the
Catholic faith as a way of helping him. However, this didn't

work out so well: As his uncle drove him to the ceremony, the boy grabbed him by the throat and screamed that the baptism wouldn't work.

THE BATTLE OF ST. LOUIS

Finally, at their wits' end, the family decided to stay with relatives in the St. Louis area. Unfortunately, the distance between Maryland and Missouri proved to be no deterrent to the invisible entity, and the assaults on Roland continued. In St. Louis, a relative introduced the boy and his family to Jesuit priest Father William Bowdern, who, in turn, employed Father Raymond J. Bishop, a pastor at St. Francis Xavier Church in St. Louis, in his efforts to help the family.

Father Bishop made several attempts to stop the attacks on the boy but to no avail. After Bishop sprinkled the boy's mattress with holy water in the shape of a cross, the attacks ceased. However, after Bishop left the room, the boy suddenly cried out in pain; when his pajama top was pulled up, Roland had numerous scratches across his abdomen. He could not have done it to himself, as he was in the presence of several witnesses at all times.

After more nights of violence against Roland, Father Bishop returned—this time with Father Bowdern. They prayed in the boy's room and then left. But as soon as they departed, loud noises began emanating from the room. When family members investigated, they found that an extremely heavy bookcase had swiveled around, a bench had overturned, and the boy's mattress was once again shaking and bouncing. It was at this point that another exorcism was deemed the only sensible course of action left.

The exorcism was a desperate battle that was waged over the course of several months. Some of it took place in the rectory at St. Francis Xavier Church, some of it at a hospital, and some of it at Roland's home. One source says that the boy was exorcised no less than 20 times.

During this time, practically everything and anything typically associated with an exorcism occurred: Roland's body jerked in uncontrollable spasms, he experienced projectile vomiting, and he spit and cursed at the priests; he also conveyed information that he couldn't possibly have known. However, his head didn't spin completely around like Linda Blair's did in *The Exorcist*.

GONE, BUT CERTAINLY NOT FORGOTTEN

Eventually, Bowdern's persistence paid off. He repeatedly practiced the ritual and ignored the torrent of physical and verbal abuse hurled at him by the entity that was residing inside the boy. Finally, in mid-April 1949, Roland spoke with a voice that identified itself as St. Michael. He ordered Satan and all demons to leave the boy alone. For the next few minutes, Roland went into a titanic rage, as if all the furies of the world were battling inside of him. Suddenly, he became quiet, turned to the priests, and simply said, "He's gone."

The entity was gone, and fortunately, Roland remembered little about the ordeal. Some months later, a 20-year-old Georgetown University student named William Peter Blatty spotted an article in *The Washington Post* about Roland's experience. He let the idea of demonic possession percolate in his brain for years before finally writing his book, which became a best seller. Out of privacy concerns, Blatty changed so many details from the actual case that the source was virtually unrecognizable—until the intense publicity surrounding the movie forced the "real" story out.

Over the years, numerous theories regarding the incident have been suggested: Some say that it was an elaborate hoax gone too far, while others claim that it was the result of poltergeist activity or an actual possession. Regardless, this case continues to resonate in American culture.

SHOCK IN THE LOCH

The legend of Nessie, the purported inhabitant of Scotland's Loch Ness, dates back to the year 565 when a roving Christian missionary named St. Columba is said to have rebuked a huge water monster to save the life of a swimmer. Rumors persisted from that time on, but it wasn't until the 20th century that the creature became internationally famous.

MONSTER AHOY

In 1933, one witness claimed he saw the creature three times; that same year, a vacationing couple claimed they saw a large creature with flippers and a long neck slither across the road and then heard it splash into the lake. These incidents made news around the world, and the hunt for Nessie was on.

Sightings multiplied and became more and more difficult to explain away. In 1971, a priest named Father Gregory Brusey saw a speedy long-necked creature cruising through the loch. One investigator estimates that more than 3,000 people have seen Nessie. The witnesses come from every walk of life, including teachers, doctors, police officers, and scientists.

MONSTER MEDIA MADNESS

As technology has advanced, Nessie has been hunted with more sophisticated equipment, always with disappointing results. In 1934, a doctor snapped the famous "Surgeon's Photo," which showed a dinosaur-like head atop a long neck sticking out of the water. The photograph has since been proven a hoax and what was thought to be Nessie was actually a picture of a toy submarine. Many other photos have been taken, but all are inconclusive.

Since 1934, numerous expeditions have been mounted in search of Nessie. Scuba divers and even submarines have scoured the lake to no avail because the amount of peat in the water makes visibility extremely poor.

In 2003, the British Broadcasting Corporation undertook a massive satellite-assisted sonar sweep of the entire lake, but again with no results. And in 2007, cameras were given to 50,000 people attending a concert on the lake's shore in hopes that someone might get lucky and snap a shot of Nessie. But apparently she doesn't like rock music—Nessie was a no-show.

Theories about Nessie's true nature abound. One of the most popular ideas, thanks to the oft-reported long neck, flippers, and bulbous body, is that Nessie is a surviving plesiosaur—a marine reptile thought to have gone extinct 65 million years ago.

Critics insist that even if a cold-blooded reptile could exist in the lake's notably frigid waters, Loch Ness is not large enough to support a breeding population of them. Other theories suggest that Nessie is a giant eel, a string of seals or otters swimming in formation, floating logs, a porpoise, an alien aquatic being, or a huge sturgeon.

Locals have repeatedly suggested that the creature is actually an aquatic demon. Stories of devil worship and mysterious rituals in the area have gone hand in hand with rumors of bodies found floating in the loch. In fact, in the early 1900s, famed occult practitioner Aleister Crowley owned a home on the lake's southern shore where he held "black masses" and conducted other ceremonies that may have aimed to "raise" monsters. And for centuries, Scots have repeated folktales of the kelpie, or water horse, a creature known to be able to shape-shift in order to lure the unwary into the water.

Whatever the truth about Nessie, she has made quite a splash as a tourist attraction. Every year thousands of people try their luck at spotting and recording the world's most famous monster.

RED EYES OVER POINT PLEASANT: THE MYSTERIOUS MOTHMAN

In 1942, the U.S. government took control of several thousand acres of land just north of Point Pleasant, West Virginia. The purpose was to build a secret facility capable of creating and storing TNT that could be used during World War II. For the next three years, the facility cranked out massive amounts of TNT, shipping it out or storing it in one of the numerous concrete "igloo" structures that dotted the area. In 1945, the facility was shut down and eventually abandoned, but it was here that an enigmatic flying creature with glowing red eyes made its home years later.

"RED EYES ON THE RIGHT"

On the evening of November 15, 1966, Linda and Roger Scarberry were out driving with another couple, Mary and Steve Mallette. As they drove, they decided to take a detour that took them past the abandoned TNT factory. As they neared the gate of the old factory, they noticed two red lights up ahead. When Roger stopped the car, the couples were horrified to find that the red lights appeared to be two glowing red eyes. What's more, those eyes belonged to a creature standing more than seven feet tall with giant wings folded behind it. That was all Roger needed to see before he hit the gas pedal and sped off. In response, the creature calmly unfolded its wings and flew toward the car. Incredibly, even though Roger raced along at speeds close to 100 miles per hour, the red-eyed creature was able to keep up with them without much effort.

Upon reaching Point Pleasant, the couples ran from their car to the courthouse and alerted Deputy Millard Halstead of their encounter. Halstead couldn't be sure exactly what the two couples had seen, but whatever it was, it had clearly frightened them. Halstead agreed to accompany them to the TNT factory. As his patrol car neared the entrance, the police radio suddenly emitted a strange, whining noise. Other than that nothing out of the ordinary was found.

MORE ENCOUNTERS

Once word got around Point Pleasant that a giant winged creature was in the area, everyone had to see it for themselves. The creature didn't disappoint. Dubbed Mothman by the press, it was spotted flying overhead, hiding, and even lurking on front porches. In fact, in the last few weeks of November, dozens of witnesses encountered the thing. But Mothman wasn't the only game in town. It seems that around the same time that he showed up, local residents started noticing strange lights in the evening sky, some of which hovered silently over the abandoned TNT factory. Of course, this led some to believe that Mothman and the UFOs were somehow connected. One such person was Mary Hyre of *The Athens Messenger*, who had been reporting on the strange activities in Point Pleasant since they started. Perhaps that's why she became the first target.

BEWARE THE MEN IN BLACK

One day, while Mary Hyre was at work, several strange men visited her office and began asking questions about the lights in the sky. Normally, she didn't mind talking to people about the UFO sightings and Mothman. But there was something peculiar about these guys. For instance, they all dressed exactly the same: black suits, black ties, black hats, and dark sunglasses. They also spoke in a strange monotone and seemed confused by ordinary objects such as ballpoint pens. By the time they left, Hyre was wondering whether they had been from another planet. Either way, she had an up-close-and-personal encounter with the legendary Men in Black.

Mary Hyre was not the only person to have a run-in with the Men in Black. As the summer of 1967 rolled around, dozens of people were interrogated by them. In most cases, the men showed up unannounced at the homes of people who had recently witnessed a Mothman or UFO sighting.

 For the most part, the men simply wanted to know what the witnesses had seen. But sometimes, the men went to great lengths to convince the witnesses that they were mistaken and had not seen anything out of the ordinary. Other times, the men threatened witnesses. Each time the Men in Black left a witness's house, they drove away in a black, unmarked sedan. Despite numerous attempts to determine who these men were and where they came from, their identity remained a secret. And all the while, the Mothman sightings continued throughout Point Pleasant and the surrounding area.

THE SILVER BRIDGE TRAGEDY

Erected in 1928, the Silver Bridge was a chain suspension bridge that spanned the Ohio River, connecting Point Pleasant with Ohio. On December 15, 1967, the bridge was busy with holiday shoppers bustling back and forth between West Virginia and Ohio. As the day wore on, more and more cars started filling the bridge until shortly before 5:00 p.m., when traffic came to a standstill. For several minutes, none of the cars budged. Suddenly, there was a loud popping noise and the unthinkable happened: The Silver Bridge collapsed, sending dozens of cars and their passengers into the freezing water below.

Over the next few days, local authorities and residents searched the river hoping to find survivors, but in the end, 46 people lost their lives in the bridge collapse. An investigation determined that a flaw in one of the bridge's supporting bars caused the collapse. But there are others who claim that in the days and weeks leading up to the collapse, they saw Mothman and even the Men in Black around, on, and even under the bridge. Further witnesses state that while most of Point Pleasant was watching the Silver Bridge collapse, bright lights and strange objects were flying out of the area and disappearing into the winter sky. Perhaps that had nothing to do with the collapse of the Silver Bridge, but the Mothman has not been seen since . . . or has he?

MOTHMAN LIVES!

There are reports that the Mothman is still alive and well and has moved on to other areas of the United States. There are even those who claim that he was spotted flying near the Twin Towers on September 11, 2001, leading to speculation that Mothman is a portent of doom. Some believe Mothman was a visitor from another planet who returned home shortly after the Silver Bridge fell. Others think the creature was the result of the toxic chemicals eventually discovered in the area near the TNT factory. And then there are skeptics who say that the initial sighting was nothing more than a giant sand crane and that mass hysteria took care of the rest.

WE TRAVELED MANY LIGHT YEARS TO HOVER OVER YOU

> **Yeah, like I'm going to call the police and say I'm John Lennon and I've seen a flying saucer.**
>
> —John Lennon

People have been seeing things in the sky for as long as there have been people. It's not that humans don't really see mysterious objects whizzing across the firmament—they do—it's the barmy conclusions they come to about those objects that entertains us the most. In former centuries there were shiny chariots and boats to bedazzle goatherds and fishermen. Shiny beings with wings were also popular. In the technologically savvy 20th century, we witnessed a proliferation of shiny discs, airships, and rockets.

Sightings aren't restricted to goatherd and fisherman types. Cops, scientists, and presidents are on record as witnessing orbs that zip around the sky pulsing with otherworldly light. And hovering. Wow do they like hovering. Our research indicates that good places to spot UFOs having a hover are deserted highways, remote rural areas, near secret government sites, and outside John Lennon's apartment.

JOHN LENNON SEES A UFO

In May 1974, former Beatle John Lennon and his assistant/
mistress May Pang returned to New York City after almost a
year's stay in Los Angeles. The pair moved into Penthouse
Tower B at 434 East 52nd Street. As Lennon watched
television on a hot summer night, he noticed flashing lights
reflected in the glass of an open door that led onto a patio. At
first dismissing it as a neon sign, Lennon suddenly realized
that since the apartment was on the roof, the glass *couldn't* be
reflecting light from the street. So—sans clothing—he ventured
onto the terrace to investigate.

SPEECHLESS

As Pang recollected, Lennon excitedly called for her to come
outside. Pang did so. "I looked up and stopped mid-sentence,"
she said later. "I couldn't even speak because I saw this thing
up there . . . it was silvery, and it was flying very slowly. There
was a white light shining around the rim and a red light on
the top . . . [it] was silent. We started to watch it drift down,
tilt slightly, and it was flying below rooftops. It was the most
amazing sight." She quickly ran back into the apartment,
grabbed her camera, and returned to the patio, clicking away.

Lennon friend and rock photography legend Bob Gruen
picked up the story: "In those days, you didn't have answering
machines, but a service [staffed by people], and I had received
a call from 'Dr. Winston.'" (Lennon's original middle name was
Winston, and he often used the alias "Dr. Winston O'Boogie.")
When Gruen returned the call, Lennon explained his incredible
sighting and insisted that the photographer come round to pick
up and develop the film personally. "He was serious," Gruen

said. "He wouldn't call me in the middle of the night to joke around." Gruen noted that although Lennon had been known to partake in mind-altering substances in the past, during this period he was totally straight. So was Pang, a nondrinker who never took drugs and whom Gruen characterized as "a clear-headed young woman."

The film in Pang's camera was a unique type supplied by Gruen, "four times as fast as the highest speed then available." Gruen had been using the film, usually employed for military reconnaissance, in low-light situations such as recording studios. The same roll already had photos of Lennon and Ringo Starr, taken during a recording session.

Gruen asked Lennon if he'd reported his sighting to the authorities. Lennon had scoffed at the idea. Gruen picked up the couple's phone and contacted the police, *The Daily News*, and the *New York Times*. The photographer claims that the cops and the *News* admitted that they'd heard similar reports, while the *Times* just hung up on him.

IT WOULD HAVE BEEN
THE ULTIMATE TRIP

Gruen's most amusing recollection of Lennon, who had been hollering "UFO!" and "Take me with you!" was that none of his NYC neighbors saw or heard the naked, ex-Beatle screaming from his penthouse terrace. And disappointingly, no one who might have piloted the craft responded to Lennon's pleas.

Gruen took the exposed film home to process, "sandwiching" it between two rolls of his own. Gruen's negatives came out perfectly, but the film Pang shot was "like a clear plastic strip," Gruen says. "We were all baffled . . . that it was completely blank." Lennon remained convinced of what he'd seen. In several shots from a subsequent photo session with Gruen that produced the iconic shot of the musician wearing a New York City T-shirt (a gift from the photographer), John points to where he'd spotted the craft. And on his *Walls and Bridges* album, Lennon wrote in the liner notes: "On the 23rd Aug. 1974 at 9 o'clock I saw a U.F.O. —J.L."

Who's to say he and May Pang didn't? Certainly not Gruen, who still declares—more than 35 years after the fact—"I believed them." And so the mystery remains.

THE MYSTERIOUS ORB

If Texas were a dartboard, the city of Brownwood would be at the center of the bull's-eye. Maybe that's how aliens saw it, too. The peaceful little city is home to about 20,000 residents and a popular train museum. A frontier town at one time, it became the trade center of Texas when the railroad arrived in 1885. Since then, the city has maintained a peaceful lifestyle. Even the massive tornado that struck Brownwood in 1976 left no fatalities. The place just has that "small town" kind of feeling.

AN INVADER FROM THE SKY

In July 2002, however, town peace was broken. Brownwood made international headlines when a strange metal orb fell from space, landed in the Colorado River, and washed up just south of town. The orb looked like a battered metal soccer ball—it was about a foot across, and it weighed just under ten pounds. Experts described it as a titanium sphere. When it was X-rayed, it revealed a second, inner sphere with tubes and wires wrapped inside.

That's all that anybody knows (or claims to know). No one is sure what the object is, and no one has claimed responsibility for it. The leading theory is that it's a cryogenic tank from some kind of spacecraft from Earth, used to store a small amount of liquid hydrogen or helium for cooling purposes. Others have speculated that it's a bomb, a spying device, or even a weapon used to combat UFOs.

IT'S NOT ALONE

The Brownwood sphere isn't unique. A similar object landed in Kingsbury, Texas, in 1997, and was quickly confiscated by the Air Force for "tests and analysis." No further announcements have been made.

Of course, the Air Force probably has a lot to keep it busy. About 200 UFOs are reported each month, and Texas is among the top states where UFOs are seen. But until anything is known for sure, those in Texas at night should keep an eye on the skies.

CLOSE ENCOUNTERS OF THE PRESIDENTIAL KIND

Not even presidents are immune from UFO sightings. During Jimmy Carter's presidential campaign of 1976, he told reporters that in 1969, before he was governor of Georgia, he saw what could have been a UFO. "It was the darndest thing I've ever seen," he said of the incident. He claimed that the object that he and a group of others had watched for ten minutes was as bright as the moon. Carter was often referred to as "the UFO president" after being elected because he filed a report on the matter.

Former actor and U.S. president Ronald Reagan witnessed UFOs on two occasions. Once during his term as California governor (1967–1975), Reagan and his wife Nancy arrived late to a party hosted by actor William Holden. Guests including Steve Allen and Lucille Ball reported that the couple excitedly described how they had just witnessed a UFO while driving along the Pacific Coast Highway. They had stopped to watch the event, which made them late to the party. Reagan also confessed to a *Wall Street Journal* reporter that in 1974, when the gubernatorial jet was preparing to land in Bakersfield, California, he noticed a strange bright light in the sky. The pilot followed the light for a short time before it suddenly shot up vertically at a high rate of speed and disappeared from sight. Reagan stopped short of labeling the light a UFO, of course. As actress Lucille Ball said in reference to Reagan's first alleged UFO sighting, "After he was elected president, I kept thinking about that event and wondered if he still would have won if he told everyone that he saw a flying saucer."

THE GREAT TEXAS AIRSHIP MYSTERY

One sunny April morning in 1897, something crashed in Aurora, Texas. Six years before the Wright Brothers' first flight and 50 years before Roswell, a huge, cigar-shaped object was seen in the skies. It was first noted on November 17,

1896, about a thousand feet above rooftops in Sacramento, California. From there, it traveled to San Francisco, where it was seen by hundreds of people.

A NATIONAL TOUR

Next, the craft apparently crossed the United States. Near Omaha, Nebraska, a farmer reported the ship on the ground, making repairs. When it returned to the skies, it headed toward Chicago, where it was photographed on April 11, 1897, the first UFO photo on record. On April 15, near Kalamazoo, Michigan, residents reported loud noises "like that of heavy ordnance" coming from the spaceship. Two days later, the UFO attempted a landing in Aurora, Texas, which should have been a good place. The town was almost deserted, and its broad, empty fields could have been an ideal landing strip.

However, at about 6 a.m. on April 17, the giant airship "sailed over the public square and, when it reached the north part of town, collided with the tower of Judge Proctor's windmill and went to pieces with a terrific explosion, scattering debris over several acres of ground, wrecking the windmill and water tank and destroying the judge's flower garden."

That's how Aurora resident and cotton buyer S. E. Haydon described the events for *The Dallas Morning News*. The remains of the ship seemed to be strips and shards of a silver-colored metal. Just one body was recovered. The newspaper reported, "while his remains are badly disfigured, enough of the original has been picked up to show that he was not an inhabitant of this world." On April 18, reportedly, that body was given a good, Christian burial in the Aurora cemetery, where it may remain to this day. A 1973 effort to exhume the body and examine it was successfully blocked by the Aurora Cemetery Association.

A FIRSTHAND ACCOUNT

Although many people have claimed the Aurora incident was a hoax, an elderly woman was interviewed in 1973 and clearly recalled the crash from her childhood. She said that her parents wouldn't let her near the debris from the spacecraft, in case it was dangerous. However, she described the alien as "a small man." Aurora continues to attract people interested in UFOs. They wonder why modern Aurora appears to be laid out like a military base. Nearby, Fort Worth seems to be home to the U.S. government's experts in alien technology. Immediately after the supposed Roswell UFO crash in 1947, it was said that debris from the spaceship was sent to Fort Worth for analysis.

The Aurora Encounter, a 1986 movie, touches on the events that began when people saw the spacecraft attempt a landing at Judge Proctor's farm. Today, the Oates gas station marks the area where the UFO crashed. Metal debris was collected from the site in the 1970s and studied by North Texas State University. That study called one fragment "most intriguing": It appeared to be iron but wasn't magnetic; it was shiny and malleable rather than brittle, as iron should be.

Today, a plaque at the Aurora cemetery mentions the spaceship, but the alien's tombstone—which, if it actually existed, is said to have featured a carved image of a spaceship—was stolen many years ago.

EXTRATERRESTRIALS PREFER CANADA

Though recorded instances of UFO sightings on Canadian soil date back to the 1950s, extraterrestrial encounters emerged most prominently on the global radar in 1967 with two startling occurrences. The first happened when a quartz prospector near a mine at Falcon Lake in Manitoba was allegedly burned by a UFO.

The second followed in October of that year at Shag Harbour, Nova Scotia, when several witnesses—including residents, the Royal Canadian Mounted Police, and an Air Canada pilot—reported strange lights hovering above the water and then submerging. A search of the site revealed only odd yellow foam, suggesting something had indeed gone underwater, but whether it was a UFO remains a mystery.

A GROWING PHENOMENON

Since then, the number of sightings in Canada has increased nearly every year. Most take place in sparsely populated regions—the rationale being that "urban glow" obscures the lights of spaceships and that country folk spend more time outdoors and thus have better opportunities to glimpse UFOs. It may also be that rural areas are simply more conducive to extraterrestrial activity. (We've heard of crop circles, but parking garage circles? Not so much.)

Most sightings reported are of the "strange light" and "weird flying vessel" variety, and indeed most have rather banal explanations (stars, airplanes, towers). Still, each year between 1 and 10 percent of sightings remain a mystery.

STRANGE LIGHTS IN MARFA

If anyone is near the southwest Texas town of Marfa at night, they should watch for odd, vivid lights over nearby Mitchell Flat. Many people believe that the lights from UFOs or even alien entities can be seen. The famous Marfa Lights are about the size of basketballs and are usually white, orange, red, or yellow. These unexplained lights only appear at night and usually hover above the ground at about shoulder height. Some of the lights—alone or in pairs—like to drift and fly around the landscape.

From cowboys to truck drivers, people traveling in Texas near the intersection of U.S. Route 90 and U.S. Route 67 have reported the Marfa Lights. And these baffling lights don't just appear on the ground. Pilots and airline passengers claim to have seen the Marfa Lights from the skies. So far, no one has provided a natural explanation for the floating orbs.

EYEWITNESS INFORMATION

Two 1988 reports were especially graphic. Pilot R. Weidig was about 8,000 feet above Marfa when he saw the lights and estimated them rising several hundred feet above the ground. Passenger E. Halsell described the lights as larger than the plane and noted that they were pulsating. In 2002, pilot B. Eubanks provided a similar report.

In addition to what can be seen, the Marfa Lights may also trigger low-frequency electromagnetic (radio) waves—which can be heard on special receivers—similar to the "whistlers" caused by lightning. However, unlike such waves from power lines and electrical storms, the Marfa whistlers are extremely loud. They can be heard as the orbs appear, and then they fade when the lights do.

A LITTLE BIT ABOUT MARFA

Marfa is about 60 miles north of the Mexican border and about 190 miles southeast of El Paso. This small, friendly Texas town is 4,800 feet above sea level and covers 1.6 square miles. In 1883, Marfa was a railroad water stop. The town grew slowly, reaching its peak during World War II when the U.S. government located a prisoner of war camp, the Marfa Army Airfield, and a chemical warfare brigade nearby. (Some skeptics suggest that discarded chemicals may be causing the Marfa Lights, but searchers have found no evidence of such.)

Today, the small town is an emerging arts center with more than a dozen artists' studios and art galleries. However, Marfa remains most famous for its light display. The annual Marfa Lights Festival is one of the town's biggest events, but the mysterious lights attract visitors year-round.

The Marfa Lights are seen almost every clear night, but they never manifest during the daytime. The lights appear between Marfa and nearby Paisano Pass, with the Chinati Mountains as a backdrop.

WIDESPREAD SIGHTINGS

The first documented sighting was by 16-year-old cowhand Robert Reed Ellison during an 1883 cattle drive. Seeing an odd light in the area, Ellison thought he'd seen an Apache campfire. When he told his story in town, however, settlers told him that they'd seen lights in the area, too, and they'd never found evidence of campfires. Two years later, 38-year-old Joe Humphreys and his wife, Sally, also reported unexplained lights at Marfa. In 1919, cowboys on a cattle drive paused to search the area for the origin of the lights. Like the others, they found no explanation for what they had seen.

In 1943, the Marfa Lights came to national attention when Fritz Kahl, an airman at the Marfa Army Base, reported that airmen were seeing lights that they couldn't explain. Four years later, he attempted to fly after them in a plane but came up empty again.

EXPLANATIONS?

Some skeptics claim that the lights are headlights from U.S. 67, dismissing the many reports from before cars—or U.S. 67—were in the Marfa area. Others insist that the lights are swamp gas, ball lightning, reflections off mica deposits, or a nightly mirage.

At the other extreme, a contingent of people believe that the floating orbs are friendly observers of life on Earth. For example, Mrs. W. T. Giddings described her father's early 20th-century encounter with the Marfa Lights. He'd become lost during a blizzard, and according to his daughter, the lights "spoke" to him and led him to a cave where he found shelter.

Most studies of the phenomenon, however, conclude that the lights are indeed real but cannot be explained. The 1989 TV show Unsolved Mysteries set up equipment to find an explanation. Scientists on the scene could only comment that the lights were not made by people.

INFAMOUS STORIES

THE BATTLE OF LOS ANGELES

On February 25, 1942, just weeks after America's entry into World War II, late-night air-raid sirens sounded a blackout throughout Los Angeles County in California. A silvery object (or objects) was spotted in the sky, prompting an all-out assault from ground troops. For an hour, antiaircraft fire bombarded the unidentified craft with some 1,400 shells, as high-powered searchlights followed its slow movement across the sky. Several witnesses reported direct hits on the invader, though it was never downed. After the "all clear" was sounded, the object vanished, and it has never been identified.

THE WASHINGTON FLAP

In two incidents just days apart in 1952, objects were seen over Washington, D.C., moving at speeds as fast as 7,000 miles per hour. At one point, separate military radar stations detected the same objects simultaneously. Eyewitnesses saw the objects from the ground and from air control towers. Three pilots spotted them at close range, saying they looked like the lit end of a cigarette or like falling stars without tails. The official Air Force explanation was "temperature inversion," and the sightings were labeled "unexplained."

FIRE IN THE SKY

After completing a job along Arizona's Mogollon Rim on November 5, 1979, Travis Walton and six fellow loggers claim they spotted a large spacecraft hovering near the dark forest road leading home. Walton approached the craft on foot and was knocked to the ground by a beam of light. Then he and the craft disappeared. Five days later, Walton mysteriously reappeared just outside of town. He said that during his time aboard the spacecraft, he had struggled to escape from the short, large-headed creatures that performed experiments on his body. Neither Walton nor any of his coworkers has strayed from the facts of their stories in nearly 30 years.

THE RENDLESHAM FOREST INCIDENT

In late December 1980, several soldiers at the Royal Air Force base in Woodbridge, Suffolk, England, saw a number of strange lights among the trees just outside their east gate. Upon investigation, they spotted a conical or disk-shaped object hovering above a clearing. The object seemed aware of their presence and moved away from them, but the men eventually gave chase. No hard evidence has been provided by the military, but the event is often considered the most significant UFO event in Britain. The Forestry Commission has since created a "UFO Trail" for hikers near the RAF base.

JAL 1628

On November 17, 1986, as Japan Airlines flight 1628 passed over Alaska, military radar detected an object on its tail. When the blip caught up with the cargo jet, the pilot reported seeing three large craft shaped like shelled walnuts, one of which was twice the size of an aircraft carrier. The objects matched the airplane's speed and tracked it for nearly an hour. At one point, the two smaller craft came so close that the pilot said he could feel their heat. The incident prompted an official FAA investigation and made worldwide headlines.

THE HILL ABDUCTION

By the 1960s, a number of people had reportedly seen
UFOs but hadn't actually encountered aliens personally.
But on September 19, 1961, Barney and Betty Hill found
themselves being chased by a spacecraft along Route 3 in
New Hampshire. The object eventually descended upon their
vehicle, whereupon Barney witnessed several humanoid
creatures through the craft's windows. The couple tried to
escape, but their car began shaking violently, and they were
forced off the road. Suffering lapses in memory from that
moment on, the Hills later recalled being taken aboard the
ship, examined, and questioned by figures with very large
eyes. The incident was known only to locals and the UFO
community until the 1966 publication of *The Interrupted
Journey* by John Fuller.

THE PHOENIX LIGHTS

In March 1997, hundreds, if not thousands, of witnesses
throughout Phoenix, Arizona, and the surrounding area
caught sight of what was to become the most controversial
UFO sighting in decades. For at least two hours, Arizona
residents watched an array of lights move across the sky,
and many reportedly saw a dark, triangular object between
them. The lights, which varied in color, were even caught on
videotape. Nearby military personnel tried to reproduce the
event by dropping flares from the sky, but most witnesses
weren't satisfied with what was deemed a diversion from
the truth.

THE MYSTERIOUS HANGAR 18

Even those who aren't UFO buffs have probably heard about the infamous Roswell Incident, where an alien spaceship supposedly crash-landed in the New Mexico desert, and the U.S. government covered the whole thing up. But what most people don't know is that according to legend, the mysterious aircraft was recovered (along with some alien bodies), secreted out of Roswell, and came to rest just outside of Dayton, Ohio.

SOMETHING CRASHED IN THE DESERT

While the exact date is unclear, some time during the first week of July 1947, a Roswell rancher by the name of Mac Brazel went out to check his property for fallen trees and other damage after a night of heavy storms and lightning. Brazel allegedly came across an area of his property littered with debris unlike anything he had ever seen before. Some of the debris even had strange writing on it.

Brazel showed some of the debris to a few neighbors and then took it to the office of Roswell sheriff George Wilcox, who called authorities at Roswell Army Air Field. After speaking with Wilcox, intelligence officer Major Jesse Marcel drove out to the Brazel ranch and collected as much debris as he could. He then returned to the airfield and showed the debris to his commanding officer, Colonel William Blanchard, commander of the 509th Bomb Group that was stationed at the Roswell Air Field. Upon seeing the debris, Blanchard dispatched military vehicles and personnel back out to the Brazel ranch to see if they could recover anything else.

"FLYING SAUCER CAPTURED!"

On July 8, 1947, Colonel Blanchard issued a press release stating that the wreckage of a "crashed disk" had been recovered. The bold headline of the July 8 edition of the *Roswell Daily Record* read: "RAAF Captures Flying Saucer on Ranch in Roswell Region." Newspapers around the world ran similar headlines. But then, within hours of the Blanchard release, General Roger M. Ramey, commander of the Eighth Air Force in Fort Worth, Texas, retracted Blanchard's release for him and issued another statement saying there was no UFO. Blanchard's men had simply recovered a fallen weather balloon. Before long, the headlines that had earlier touted the capture of a UFO read: "It's a Weather Balloon" and "'Flying Disc' Turns Up as Just Hot Air." Later editions even ran a staged photograph of Major Jesse Marcel, who was first sent to investigate the incident, kneeling in front of weather balloon debris. Most of the general public seemed content with the explanation, but there were skeptics.

WHISKED AWAY TO HANGAR 18?

Those who believe that aliens crash-landed near Roswell claim that, under cover of darkness, large portions of the alien spacecraft were brought out to the Roswell Air Field and loaded onto B-29 and C-54 aircrafts. Those planes were then supposedly flown to Wright-Patterson Air Force Base, just outside of Dayton. Once the planes landed, they were taxied over to Hangar 18 and unloaded. And according to legend, it's all still there.

There are some problems with the story, though. For one, none of the hangars on Wright-Patterson Air Force Base are officially known as "Hangar 18," and there are no buildings designated with the number 18. Rather, the hangars are labeled 1A, 1B, 1C, and so on. There's also the fact that none of the hangars seem large enough to house and conceal an alien spacecraft. But just because there's nothing listed as Hangar 18 on a Wright-Patterson map doesn't mean it's not there. Conspiracy theorists believe that hangars 4A, 4B, and 4C might be the infamous Hangar 18. As for the size of the hangars, it's believed that most of the wreckage has been stored in giant tunnels and chambers under the hangar, to protect the debris and to keep it safe from prying eyes. It is said that Wright-Patterson is conducting experiments on the wreckage to see if scientists can reverse-engineer the technology.

SO WHAT'S THE DEAL?

The Hangar 18 story got stranger as the years went on, starting with the government's Project Blue Book, a program designed to investigate reported UFO sightings. Between 1947 and 1969, Project Blue Book investigated more than 12,000 sightings before being disbanded. And where was Project Blue Book headquartered? Wright-Patterson Air Force Base. Then in the early 1960s, senator Barry Goldwater, himself a retired major general in the U.S. Army Air Corps (and friend of Colonel Blanchard), became interested in what had crashed in Roswell. When Goldwater discovered Hangar 18, he wrote to Wright-Patterson and asked for permission to tour the facility but was denied. He then approached another friend, General Curtis LeMay, and asked if he could see the "Green Room" where the UFO was being held. Goldwater claimed that LeMay gave him "holy hell" and screamed at Goldwater, "Not only can't you get into it, but don't you ever mention it to me again."

Most recently, in 1982, retired pilot Oliver "Pappy" Henderson attended a reunion and announced that he was one of the men who had flown alien bodies out of Roswell in a C-54 cargo plane. His destination? Hangar 18 at Wright-Patterson. Although no one is closer to a definitive answer, it seems that the legend of Hangar 18 will never die.

AVROCAR: THE GOVERNMENT'S HOMEMADE UFO

At a time when UFO enthusiasm was at full boil, the U.S. government decided to start a top-secret program to create saucer-shaped flying machines.

Oh, the 1950s—a time of sock hops, drive-in movies, and the Cold War between America and the Soviet Union, when each superpower waged war against the other in the arenas of scientific technology, astronomy, and politics. It was also a time when discussion of life on other planets was rampant, fueled by the alleged crash near Roswell.

WATCH THE SKIES

For a while, it seemed like everyone, from farmers to airplane pilots, was spotting UFOs over the good old USA. As time passed, government authorities began to wonder if the flying saucers were, in fact, part of a secret Russian program to create a new type of air force. Fearful that such a craft would upset the balance of power, the U.S. Air Force decided to produce its own saucer ship.

In 1953, the military contacted Avro Aircraft Limited of Canada, an aircraft manufacturing company that operated in Malton, Ontario, between 1945 and 1962. Project Silverbug was initially proposed simply because the government wanted to find out if UFOs could be made by humans. But before long, both the military and the scientific community were speculating about its potential. Intrigued, designers at Avro—led by British engineer John Frost—began working on the VZ-9-AV Avrocar. The craft would have been right at home in a scene from the science fiction film *The Day the Earth Stood Still*. Security for the project was so tight that it probably generated rumors that America was actually testing a captured alien spacecraft—speculation that remains alive and well even today.

OF THIS EARTH

By 1958, the company had two prototypes, which were 18 feet in diameter and 3.5 feet tall. Constructed around a large triangle, the Avrocar was shaped like a disk, with a curved upper surface. It included an enclosed 124-blade turbo-rotor at the center of the triangle, which provided lifting power through an opening in the bottom of the craft. The turbo also powered the craft's controls. Although conceived as being able to carry two passengers, in reality a single pilot could barely fit inside the cramped space. The Avrocar was operated with a single control stick, which activated different panels around the ship. Airflow issued from a large center ring, which was controlled by the pilot to guide the craft either vertically or horizontally.

The military envisioned using the craft as "flying Jeeps" that would hover close to the ground. But that, apparently, was only going to be the beginning. Avro had its own plans, which included not just commercial Avrocars, but also a family-size Avrowagon, an Avrotruck for larger loads, Avroangel to rush people to the hospital, and a military Avropelican, which, like a pelican hunting for fish, would search for submarines.

BUT DOES IT FLY?

The prototypes impressed the U.S. Army enough to award Avro a $2 million contract. Unfortunately, the Avrocar project was canceled when an economic downturn forced the company to temporarily close and restructure. When Avro Aircraft reopened, the original team of designers had dispersed. Further efforts to revive the project were unsuccessful, and repeated testing proved that the craft was inherently unstable. Project Silverbug was abandoned when funding ran out in March 1961, but one of the two Avrocar prototypes is housed at the U.S. Army Transportation Museum in Fort Eustis, Virginia.

WHAT'S UP WITH AREA 51?

It's the mystery spot to end all mystery spots. Speculation about its purpose has run the gamut from a top-secret test range to an alien research center. One thing is certain—the truth is out there somewhere.

Located near the southern shore of the dry lakebed known as Groom Lake is a large military airfield—one of the most secretive places in the country. It is fairly isolated from the outside world, and little official information has ever been published on it. The area is not included on any maps, yet nearby Nevada state route 375 is listed as "The Extraterrestrial Highway." Although referred to by a variety of names, including Dreamland, Paradise Ranch, Watertown Strip, and Homey Airport, this tract of mysterious land in southern Nevada is most commonly known as "Area 51." Conspiracy theorists and UFO aficionados speculate that Area 51 is everything from the storage location of the rumored crashed Roswell, New Mexico, spacecraft to a secret lab where experiments are conducted on matter transportation and time travel.

The truth is far less fantastic and probably far more scientific. Used as a bomb range during World War II, the site was abandoned as a military base at the end of the war. So much for being home to that alien spacecraft from Roswell. The land wasn't used again until 1955, when the site became a test range for the Lockheed U-2 spy plane and, later, the USAF SR-71 Blackbird.

Was Area 51 ever used to house UFOs? Don't bet your paycheck on it. But experts believe that the site at Groom Lake was probably a test and study center for captured Soviet aircraft during the Cold War. In 2003, the federal government actually admitted the facility exists as an Air Force "operating location," but no further information was released. Today, the area, including the various runways, is officially designated as "Homey Airport."